KCDX 2
赤松健
KEN AKAMATSU
AIが止まらない!
新装版
02

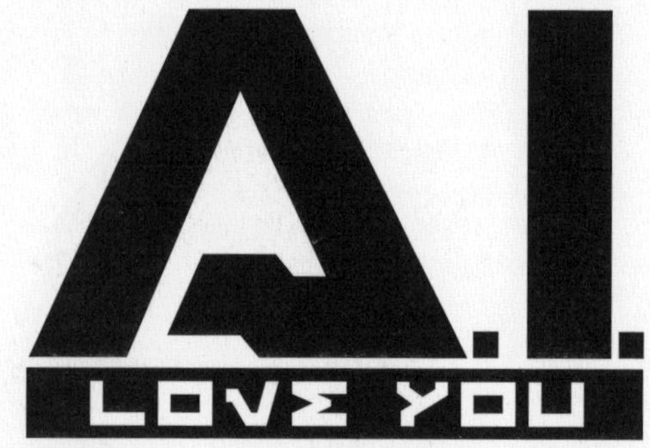

BY
KEN AKAMATSU

volume
2

LOS ANGELES • TOKYO • LONDON

Translator - David Ury
English Adaptation - Adam Arnold
Layout and Lettering - Steven Redd
Copy Editor- Aaron Sparrow
Cover Layout - Patrick Hook

Editor - Rob Tokar
Digital Imaging Manager - Chris Buford
Pre-Press Manager - Antonio DePietro
Production Managers - Jennifer Miller, Mutsumi Miyazaki
Art Director - Matt Alford
Managing Editor - Jill Freshney
VP of Production - Ron Klamert
President & C.O.O. - John Parker
Publisher & C.E.O. - Stuart Levy

E-mail: info@TOKYOPOP.com

Come visit us online at www.TOKYOPOP.com

A  Manga

TOKYOPOP Inc.
5900 Wilshire Blvd. Suite 2000
Los Angeles, CA 90036

A.I. Love You Vol. 2

ISBN: 1-59182-616-0

First TOKYOPOP printing: April 2004

10 9 8 7 6 5 4 3 2 1

Printed in the USA

Program.

Story So Far

Hitoshi Kobe is a poor student, a bad athlete and may be the unluckiest man alive. Hitoshi's parents are high-level programmers for an American company and they spend most of the year living and working abroad. As a result, Hitoshi gets unrestricted access to the equipment his parents left in their home. Whenever Hitoshi has the chance, he uses his folks' high-tech gear to work on making new friends--literally!

Unknown to most people, Hitoshi has an unbelievable knack for creating Artificial Intelligence programs. Routinely picked on, put down, and tricked by his peers, it's no wonder that Hitoshi's closest friend is Number Thirty (also known as Saati), an A.I. he created himself. Hitoshi and Thirty get along so well, in fact, that they promised to be boyfriend and girlfriend if Saati should ever become a real girl. Their seemingly idle promise was quickly put to the test when a freak lightning storm somehow gave Saati the ability to leave the computer and become real!

Though she looks like a human girl, Saati still has many of the advantages of a computer program...and some extra abilities as well! Unfortunately for Hitoshi, cooking is not one of them. Saati doesn't **cook** meals, she **makes** them...out of clay, paints, and whatever else she can find that will help her match the picture of the recipe.

However, Saati more than makes up for her kitchen catastrophes by being Hitoshi's number one (and only) fan and supporter. On the first day that Saati came to school with Hitoshi, she told everyone she was Hitoshi's live-in girlfriend and made Hitoshi the envy of every guy in his class. In addition, thanks Saati's intervention, Hitoshi shined in front of his math class, scored a goal in gym class, and defeated the latest in a series of embarrassing pranks without even trying.

Since Saati became real, Hitoshi's life has become much more interesting than he ever could have hoped...and it's only getting wilder!

CONTENTS

Program.8

Happy (Or Unhappy) Birthday

* This story is a work of fiction and has no connection with actual living people or organizations.

HEY, HITOSHI, MY MAN!
TELL US, DUDE. WHAT'S SAATI'S BIRTHDAY, HUH?

EH? HER BIRTHDAY?

YEAH, WE WANTED TO THROW HER A LITTLE BASH. SHOW HER WE CARE.
A GIRL'S BIRTHDAY IS A BIG DEAL, AFTER ALL.
SO TRUE.
BIRTHDA

OKAY, SAATI'S BIRTHDAY IS...
...UMM...

I GUESS THAT WOULD BE THE DAY SHE CAME OUT OF THE COMPUTER.

I'M PRETTY SURE IT'S APRIL 6TH.
WHAT?!
YOU MEAN IT'S ALREADY PASSED?

DID YOU THROW HER A PARTY?
UH...NO.

YOU DUMBASS!
YOU GOTTA *DO* STUFF LIKE THAT! IF NOT, SHE'LL FIND SOMEBODY ELSE!
EXACTLY!

WHA--?!

I STILL DON'T SEE WHY SHE'S WITH YOU, ANYWAY.
SHE'LL DUMP YOU IF YOU'RE NOT CAREFUL.

WHAT IF...
...WHAT IF THEY'RE RIGHT?

ガタ
ガタ

THAT REMINDS ME. IT'S ALMOST JUNE 5TH.
MY BIRTHDAY'S COMING UP.

BUT WHAT'S IT MATTER? BIRTHDAYS AND ME JUST DON'T MESH.

IN ELEMENTARY SCHOOL...
...I NEVER EVEN GOT INVITED TO A SINGLE GIRL'S PARTY.
IN JUNIOR HIGH, MY PARENTS WERE ALWAYS BUSY.
SO, I'D ALWAYS END UP ALONE WITH SOME STORE-BOUGHT CAKE.

I CAN'T EVEN RECALL A SINGLE ENJOYABLE BIRTHDAY IN 15 YEARS.

...BUT THIS YEAR WILL BE DIFFERENT!!
THIS TIME...I HAVE A GIRLFRIEND!!

AND WE CAN CELEBRATE MY BIRTHDAY TOGETHER.
HAPPY BIRTHDAY, HITOSHI-SAN.
THANKS, SAATI.

SO, YOU'RE FINALLY A MAN NOW.
HUH?

I'M SORRY I DIDN'T GET YOU ANYTHING.
BUT IF YOU LIKE, YOU CAN HAVE ME.
SA-SAATI, IT'S MY--
MINE TOO.
ゴッ
OW! MY NOSE!!
I'VE GOTTA GET AHOLD OF MYSELF.
OWW.
FIRST THINGS FIRST...I NEED TO LET SAATI KNOW ABOUT MY BIRTHDAY.
キョロ
キョロ
UM, WHERE IS SHE?

YOU SEEN SAATI AROUND?
SAATI? UM, SHE WENT HOME.

WHAT?
SHE LEFT BEFORE ME?

HEY, SAATI.
WHY'D YOU COME HOME EARLY TODAY?

......
Totally Spaced Out

IS SOMETHING THE MATTER?

O-OKAY, GOT IT!!

ANOTHER 30 SERVINGS, RIGHT?!
THERE YOU GO!

UM, IS SOME-THING WRONG WITH YOU?
HUH?

NO. THERE'S NOTHING...
...WRONG WITH ME.

....
REALLY?

MAYBE IT'S JUST ME.
BUT IS SHE ACTING KIND OF WEIRD?

WHAT IF SHE'S GETTING SICK AGAIN?
HEY, SAATI. GOT A MINUTE?

SAATI?
ARE YOU IN THERE?
YEAH, JUST A SECOND!

IS SHE IN THE BATH-ROOM?
WHAT ARE YOU DOING? I'M COMING IN.
ガチャ
ホッ

!!

AAAAHH!

GET OUT OF HERE!

YOU PERVERT!

ゴン

OKAY, OKAY! I'M SORRY! OWW!

ごち

OH, JEEZ. I'VE REALLY DONE IT NOW!
IT'S NOT FAIR! WHY IS THIS ALWAYS HAPPENING TO ME?!

SAATI, I'M REALLY SORRY.
PLEASE, DON'T BE MAD.
LISTEN, I WANTED--
NO! DON'T COME IN HERE!!
ガタガタン

IT'S ALL RIGHT. I'M NOT MAD ABOUT WHAT HAPPENED.
SO, UM, THAT'S IT. 'NIGHT.
バタン
UH, YEAH. GOOD NIGHT.
AH, CRAP! SHE MUST BE REALLY PISSED NOW!
SHE EVEN FLIPPED OUT OVER ME WALKING IN ON HER!
I HAVE TO APOLOGIZE TOMORROW...
...OR I WON'T EVER HAVE A PARTY.
The next day...
YAAAHH! I COULDN'T EVEN GET TO SLEEP LAST NIGHT.
HUH?
I'M GOING OUT. - SAATI
WHAT THE HECK?!

"I'M GOING OUT?!"
WHAT? IS SHE RUNNING AWAY?!

SHE WOULDN'T LEAVE BECAUSE I WALKED IN ON HER... WOULD SHE?
THEN AGAIN, SHE HAS BEEN TRYING TO ACT MORE LIKE A NORMAL PERSON LATELY.

NO, THAT CAN'T BE IT! IT'S ME!!
WHAT DO I DO?!
だん
だんだん
だん

STILL, SHE HAS BEEN SPENDING A LOT OF TIME IN HER ROOM LATELY.

EITHER SHE'S, YOU KNOW... OR SHE'S PURPOSELY TRYING TO AVOID ME.

UGH, NOW I'M SO WORRIED I CAN'T EVEN THINK STRAIGHT.

ガチャ
I'M HOME!

SAATI!
WHAT WERE YOU DOING OUT AT THIS HOUR?
UH, NOTHING.
サッ
I JUST, UH, WENT OUT.

UM, EXCUSE ME, THERE'S SOMETHING I HAVE TO DO.
カチャ
HUH? WAIT A SE--
バタン

I DON'T GET IT, SAATI.
WHAT THE HECK HAS GOTTEN INTO YOU?

And then, Hitoshi's birthday arrived...
チュン
チュン
ウロ
ウロ

BIRTHDAY OR NOT, THIS CAN'T GO ON.
I HAVE TO APOLOGIZE TODAY.

AH, SAATI!
カチャッ

HUH, YOU'RE DRESSED?
YOU GOING OUT AGAIN?

YEAH. THERE'S SOMEONE I WANT TO SEE.
I'LL SEE YOU LATER, HITOSHI-SAN.

!!
IF NOT, SHE'LL FIND SOMEBODY ELSE!
DON'T SEE WHY SHE'S WITH YOU ANYWAY.

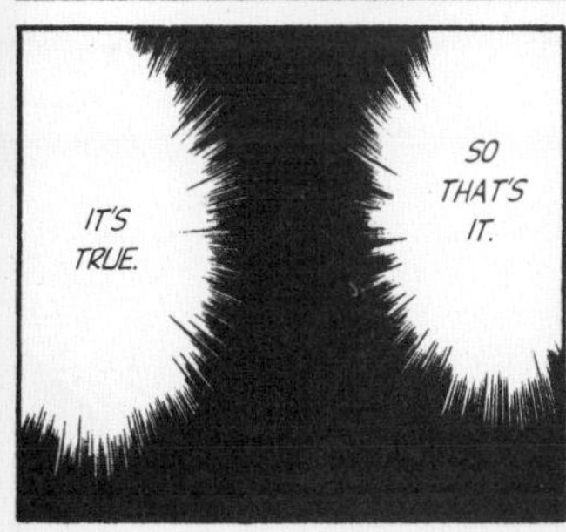
SO THAT'S IT.
IT'S TRUE.

SAATI'S BEEN...
...SEEING ANOTHER GUY!!

COVENT GARDEN
Mizuno Accounting Office
SHE'S BUYING FLOWERS?
BUT...FOR WHOM?
AND WHAT ABOUT THAT BAG UNDER HER ARM?
IS THAT SOME PRESENT FOR HIM?
1-Hour Photo
K
No minimum!
Gift Certificates Available
WAIT, WOULD SAATI REALLY GO OUT WITH ANOTHER GUY?
I MEAN, I'M HER BOYFRIEND, AREN'T I?
SHE HAS BECOME AWFULLY HUMAN LATELY.
LIKING SOMEONE ELSE WOULDN'T BE OUT OF THE QUESTION.

HEY, SENSEI!
WHA?!
I KNEW IT!
HOW ARE YOU?
PRETTY GOOD. YOU?
Anything
From Asia
SHE LOOKS SO HAPPY.
I GUESS THAT'S THE GUY.
THIS IS THE GIFT I WAS TALKING ABOUT.
AH, LET'S HAVE A LOOK.
....
IT'S OVER. SAATI'S LEFT ME.
?

GRAND PONT
グランポン
GRAND PONT
¥1,000
¥2,000

SAATI, I... I DIDN'T KNOW.
WHY DIDN'T YOU TELL ME?
よろっ
HUH?
HEH.

I, UH, I'M NOT T-TRYING TO HOLD YOU BACK.
IF YOU LIKE SOMEONE ELSE, SAATI... IT'S OKAY.
I WON'T GET IN YOUR WAY.

HAVE A GOOD LIFE TOGETHER!!
ダッ
HITOSHI-SAN! WAIT!!
POINT
I'M SORRY. I HAVE GO AFTER HIM!
UM, PLEASE DO.
Anything
From Asia
HITOSHI-SAN, WHERE DID YOU GO?
HEY, SAATI!!
HUH? ASO-SAN?
WHAT'S WRONG WITH KOBE-KUN? HE LOOKED LIKE HE WAS GONNA KILL HIMSELF.
DID YOU GUYS HAVE A FIGHT?

KILL HIMSELF?
WHY WOULD HE...?
ギュッ
ザッ
HITOSHI-SAN!!
ダッ
WHAT'S UP WITH THOSE TWO?
IF HITOSHI-SAN ISN'T AROUND ANYMORE, THEN WHAT'LL I DO?
HITOSHI-SAN!
I'LL BE ALL... ALONE.

PROGRAM OPTION NUMBER THREE!!
MAGNIFY HEARING TO MAXIMUM DECIBEL LEVELS!
PLEASE, HITOSHI-SAN...
...PLEASE BE ALIVE.
NOPE.
ガヤガヤ
ガヤ
NOT HIM EITHER.
パパーッ
ドクン...
ドクン...
THAT SOUND!!
ドクン...
THAT'S HIM! THAT'S HITOSHI'S HEARTBEAT!!
AAAHH.
ポチャン
UGHH.
GOD, THIS BIRTHDAY SUCKS TOO.
AW, WHY DO I EVEN CARE ANYMORE?
HITOSHI-SAN!!

バチ
チッ
まんじゅう
SAATI?!
Pant
Pant

HITOSHI-SAN, TODAY'S YOUR BIRTHDAY, RIGHT?
ハァハァ
I HAD SOMETHING I WANTED TO GIVE YOU.

WHAT?!
YOU KNEW?!

HERE. I MADE THIS FOR YOU.
ハァハァ
I WANTED TO SURPRISE YOU, BUT IT'S OKAY.

A HAND-KNIT SWEATER?
SO THAT WAS THE REASON. SHE WAS MAKING THIS ALL ALONG.

I COULDN'T GET IT QUITE RIGHT, SO I'VE BEEN TAKING A CLASS.

EHEH HEH. SO, IT WAS ALL...
...JUST A BIG MISUNDER-STANDING THEN?
PHEW! THAT'S A RELIEF.
ヘニャ ヘニャ〜
NO, DON'T JUMP!!
WHA?!
ドッパーン
THANKS, SAATI.
ハハハ
ハハハ
THIS IS THE BEST PRESENT I'VE EVER GOTTEN.
でろ〜ん
......
パチパチ
AWWW! IT LOOKS PERFECT ON YOU!!

Hitoshi is, quite simply, a programming genius. His intellect is far superior to even that of Bill Gates, but you probably would not be able to guess that from looking at him. Though he has written many programs, he's always been a loner. Saati is the one who finally managed to break through to Hitoshi and show him how to live.

Program.9

The Good Life

* Gyu-tan-yaki - Grilled Beef Tongue.

WHAT THE? THESE THINGS THAT LOOK LIKE CARROTS ARE ACTUALLY HOT PEPPERS! WHAT THE?! WHY ARE THERE HOT PEPPERS THAT LOOK LIKE CARROTS?!
UM, I DIDN'T HAVE THE RIGHT COLOR, SO I--

UGH, SAATI. IT'S BEEN TWO MONTHS...
AT LEAST THERE ARE INSTANT NOODLES.
...AND YOUR COOKING *STILL* HASN'T GOTTEN ANY BETTER.

I'M SORRY, HITOSHI-SAN.

I USE RICE AND RAW TOPPINGS?
HMM, I SEE.

I KNOW SAATI IS TRYING...
...BUT AT THIS RATE, I'LL STARVE TO DEATH FIRST.

MAYBE SHE NEEDS COOKING LESSONS.
YEAH, THAT'LL WORK!

AH, THIS IS THE PLACE.
IT'S HUMONGOUS!
YEP, ALL OF THE FAMOUS CHEFS LIVE AROUND HERE.
I'M SURE ONE OF THEM CAN HELP YOU.
A FAMOUS CHEF TEACHING ME?!
UH, IT MIGHT NOT BE THAT EASY, SAATI.
OBSTINATE IS WHAT THEY ARE.
OBSTIN-ATE? IS THAT A CLUB?
Obstinate Club
THEY'RE ALSO STUBBORN.
THEY STUB THEIR TOES A LOT?
AND THEY'RE KNOWN FOR BEING HEART-LESS DEMONS!
THAT SOUNDS AWFUL!
LEAVE NOW, MORTAL!
AHHH!
NOT TO MENTION THEY'RE PROBABLY SO OLD THEY FORGOT HOW TO COOK!
ははははは
YOU BETTER WATCH YOUR MOUTH, SONNY.
?!
DON'T PLAY WITH ME.
WHAT THE HELL DO YOU KIDS WANT?

WWAARGGH?!
OHH, SO THIS IS A FAMOUS CHEF?
LOOKS DIFFERENT THAN I EXPECTED.
YOU JUST WANT TO LEARN BECAUSE IT'S HIP.
WELL, I WOULDN'T BE CAUGHT DEAD TEACHING YOU!
フン
WHAT?!
BUT WHY?!
YOU YOUNG PEOPLE DON'T KNOW A BEAN FROM A BEAN SPROUT!
CAN'T TEACH YOU NOTHIN'!
PLEASE, MA'AM! I'LL TRY MY HARDEST!
HMMM.
WELL, I MIGHT LET YOU STICK AROUND...IF YOU CLEAN MY HOUSE FIRST.
WHAT?! THIS HUGE PLACE? BUT THAT'S IMPOSSIBLE!!
IF IT'S IMPOSSIBLE, THEN GO HOME, RUNT.
THAT STUPID OLD HAG!
SENSEI!
むむむ

LOOK, SENSEI! I DID IT!!
ペカーっ
W-WHAT THE?!
BUT HOW DID YOU--?!
ALL RIGHT, SAATI!! JACKPOT!!
HMMMM.
WELL, I GUESS YOU CAN STICK AROUND, THEN.
THANK YOU, SENSEI!!
HERE, THIS IS THE KITCHEN.
HUH?!

WAIT A SEC, NO GAS...OR ELECTRICITY?
DON'T TELL ME YOU USE A WOOD-BURNING STOVE?!
YOU SURE COMPLAIN A LOT.
IN THE OLD DAYS, THIS IS HOW WE ALL COOKED.
AH, YOU'RE BACK. LET'S START BY TESTING YOUR SKILLS.
ガサゴソ
HMMM
SURE, WHAT SHOULD I DO?
PURU PURU
でん～
WHY DON'T YOU SLICE THIS RADISH UP FOR ME?
THAT SOUNDS EASY ENOUGH!
LET'S GIVE IT A TRY!
NOW STAND BACK, OKAY?!
?!
PURU PURU

INITIATE SCANNING! LENGTH: 422.159 CM. DIAMETER: 8.510 CM.
MAXIMIZING DIMENSIONAL RADISH USAGE. ANALYSIS COMPLETE.

THE RADISH IS SLICED!
AND... VOILA!
PURU PURU

UM, SAATI? I DON'T THINK YOU'RE MAKING NOODLES.
BUT I WASN'T!
WHAT IS IT WITH THESE KIDS?

OKAY, HOW ABOUT I JUST BREAK THEM IN HALF?
THAT SHOULD SOLVE THE PROBLEM!
STOP PLAYING WITH THE FOOD!!

MORE IMPORTANTLY, WHO IN THE HELL USES A RAZOR BLADE FOR COOKING, HUH?!
WHAT? IS THERE SOMETHING WRONG WITH THAT?

UGH, I GIVE UP.
WHAT DID YOU WANT TO MAKE?

UM, CURRY RICE, PLEASE. I EVEN BROUGHT ALONG THE INGREDIENTS.

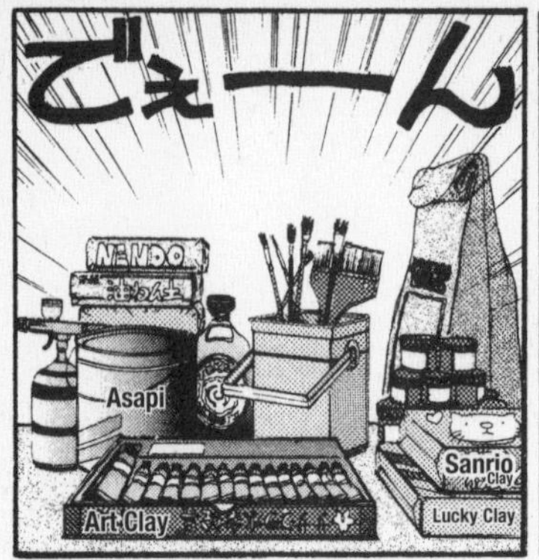
でえーーん
NENDO
Asapi
Sanrio Clay
Lucky Clay
Art Clay

Y-YOU'RE GOING TO MAKE CURRY RICE WITH...THIS?

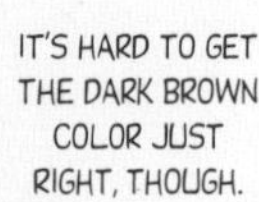
IT'S HARD TO GET THE DARK BROWN COLOR JUST RIGHT, THOUGH.

I MAKE THE SAUCE WITH SOFT CLAY AND SOME OTHER TOPPINGS.
THE RICE PART ONLY HAS TO LOOK WHITE, SO I--
RUBBER ERASER
ROCK
STYROFOAM
SOAP
PING PONG BALL
CLAY
IT'S A CURRY

ARE YOU KIDS SCREWIN' WITH ME?!
DID I DO SOME-THING WRONG?

CURRY IS MEAT, VEGETABLES AND POWDER. NOT SOME DAMN PHOTO-OP! NOW WATCH!

ショリョショリョショリョ

トントン
トン
MAN, SHE'S A REAL PRO!
WOW! SO THAT'S HOW YOU DO IT.
トン

YOU MEAN LIKE THIS?

THIS PART IS JUST COMMON SENSE. UNDERSTAND?

バーン

WHAT ARE YOU TRYING TO FEED, AN ARMY?! DON'T PEEL SO MANY!

OOPS... SORRY.

I CAN'T TELL IF SHE'S PLAYING WITH ME OR IF SHE'S SERIOUS.

グッグッ

NOW WE ADD THE MEAT.
GOT IT!
OH...THE MEAT GOES IN LIKE THIS...

MMM. THAT SURE SMELLS GOOD.

NOW, THIS IS WHERE IT GETS TRICKY.
ぐつぐつ
YOU LET IT SIMMER FOR TWO TO THREE HOURS AND STIR IT OCCASIONALLY SO IT DOESN'T BURN.

GOT IT?
YES, MA'AM!!

I'M GOING TO GO REST MY EYES. STIR MINE ALSO, PLEASE.
SURE THING!
JUST KEEP STIRRING.
ぐつ
ぐつ
ぐつ
ぐつ
ゴーッ
パチパチ
PHEW!
IT'S SO HOT.
PURU PURU
グツ
グツ
グツ
....
I HOPE SHE'LL BE ALL RIGHT.
IF SHE STANDS BY THAT HOT STOVE TOO LONG, SHE MIGHT OVERHEAT.
Modern

UM, SENSEI? HOW MUCH LONGER DOES SHE HAVE TO STIR THAT?
HMM?
トポポポ
ABOUT TWO MORE HOURS I RECKON'.
TWO MORE HOURS?!
SAATI, YOU MUST BE HOT! WHY DON'T YOU LET ME STIR FOR YOU?
THAT'S OKAY! I'M FINE, THANKS.
Modern
PURU PURU
ARE YOU SURE, SAATI? YOU SEEM KIND OF FEVERISH.
I'M OKAY, HITOSHI-SAN.
I CAN HANDLE IT MYSELF.
UH, OKAY.
HEY YOU! QUIT BOTHERIN' THE COOK!

GO CHOP SOME FIREWOOD OR SOMETHIN' USEFUL.
FIREWOOD?!
WHAT DO I LOOK LIKE, A LUMBERJACK?
Sun Rice
Shima Brand
くすっ
......
I'M SORRY, HITOSHI-SAN. IT'S JUST THAT...
ぐつ ぐつ
...FOR ONCE I'D LIKE TO MAKE YOU SOMETHING DELICIOUS ALL BY MYSELF.
JUST ONCE...
...I'D LIKE TO SEE YOU SMILE WHEN YOU TRY MY COOKING.
HMMM.
THAT GIRL'S BEEN STANDIN' THERE FOR QUITE SOME TIME.
コト コト
PURU PURU
グツ グツ グツ グツ
I THINK THAT'S ABOUT RIGHT.

チュ
HOW'S IT TASTE?
GOOD...?
IT'S PROBABLY JUST ABOUT READY.
GO AHEAD AND SERVE SOME UP.
ジャーン
WHOA, SAATI!
THAT LOOKS *AMAZING!!*
NOT ONLY THAT, IT *SMELLS* GREAT TOO!
THIS MIGHT ACTUALLY BE GOOD.
ドキドキドキドキ
......
WELL, LET'S HAVE A TASTE!
Modern

ゴバァァァァッ

AHHH--

AAARGHH! SPICY SPICY! HOT HOT HOT!!
WHAT? THAT DOESN'T MAKE ANY SENSE!
MY CURRY TURNED OUT JUST FINE.
ぱくっ
......
B-BUT... HOW?
だーっ

YOU TASTED IT BEFORE YOU SERVED IT, RIGHT?!
HOW COULD YOU NOT NOTICE?!

I...I'M NOT SURE.
I'M SORRY, SENSEI.

YOU USED THE SAME INGREDIENTS AND TECHNIQUE AS ME.

I DON'T UNDERSTAND WHAT COULD'VE GONE WRONG.

WHAT'S WRONG WITH SAATI'S TONGUE?

WHOA! HOLD UP!

DOES SAATI EVEN HAVE ANY TASTE BUDS?

TASTE BUDS

SAATI, DO ME A FAVOR. TASTE SOME OF THIS SALT.
HUH?
食塩
JT

WHAT'S IT TASTE LIKE?
....

LETS SEE, IT'S MADE UP OF THE CHEMICAL COMPOUND SODIUM CHLORIDE...
...THEREFORE, THEORETICALLY, IT MUST BE SALTY!
PURU PURU

OH, CRAP!!
I KNEW IT!
Modern

SAATI HAS NO CONCEPT OF SWEET, SALTY OR SPICY.
The Great Taste Test
Sweet
Spicy
Salty
Bitter
I GUESS I FORGOT TO PROGRAM HER WITH A SENSE OF TASTE.

カチャ
HERE, READ THE FILE "TASTE.COM."
THEN AT LEAST YOU'LL UNDERSTAND WHAT TASTE IS.
"TASTE.COM," RIGHT?
Modern

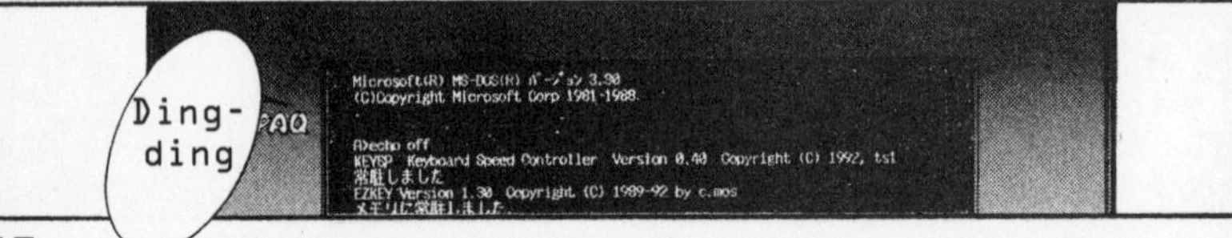
Ding-ding
Microsoft(R) MS-DOS(R) バージョン 3.30
(C)Copyright Microsoft Corp 1981-1988.
A>echo off
KEYSP Keyboard Speed Controller Version 0.40 Copyright (C) 1992, tsl
常駐しました
EZKEY Version 1.30 Copyright (C) 1989-92 by c.mos

ALL FINISH-ED.
IS THAT IT FOR NOW?
YEAH, THAT'S IT.
SO...FEEL ANY DIFFERENT?
Modern
PURU PURU
HMM. I'M NOT REALLY SURE YET.
MAYBE.
HUH?
YOU WANT ME TO TEACH YOU AGAIN?
I KNOW THIS TIME I CAN MAKE THE PERFECT CURRY RICE!
SO PLEASE, SENSEI...TEACH ME AGAIN!
PURU PURU
JUST FORGET ABOUT IT. CURRY IS TOO HARD FOR YOU.
I DON'T SEE WHY YOU'RE SO OBSESSED WITH CURRY.
THERE ARE PLENTY OF OTHER DISHES OUT THERE.
WELL, YOU SEE...
PURU PURU

...IT'S JUST THAT...
...HITOSHI-SAN'S FAVORITE MEAL IS CURRY RICE.

......
やれやれ
WELL, WELL...

I SUPPOSE I CAN SHOW YOU ONE MORE TIME.
THANK YOU SO MUCH, SENSEI!

で〜〜ん

UMM...
ごくっ
...IS THIS EVEN EDIBLE?

......
ドキ
ドキ
ドキ
ALL RIGHT, I'LL GIVE IT A TRY.
PLEASE GO AHEAD!

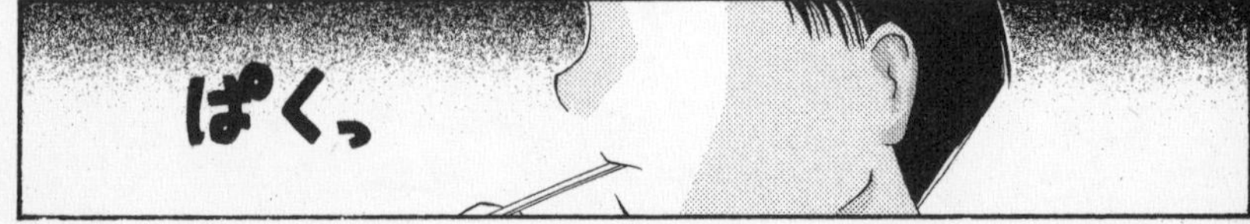
ぱくっ

AHHH!!
OH!
THIS TASTES GREAT!
!
ABSOLUTELY!
I THINK YOU'VE GOT IT THIS TIME!
....
YOU REALLY MEAN IT?
WHAT DO YOU THINK, SENSEI?!
THIS IS PRETTY GOOD, ISN'T IT?!
ぱくっ
もぐもぐ
HMM. WELL...
PU
URU

YES! I FINALLY DID IT!
LOVE IS THE MOST IMPORTANT INGREDIENT, AFTER ALL.
...AFTER ALL THAT EFFORT, IT HAS TO TASTE GOOD.
SENSEI!?
THANKS FOR ALL THE HELP.
YOU KNOW, KID, YOU'VE CAUGHT YOURSELF A VERY NICE GIRL THERE!
MIGHT BE A BIT *TOO* GOOD FOR YOU, THOUGH!
STICK TO THE COOKING LADY!
HITOSHI-SAN, BREAK-FAST IS READY!
AND THUS, SAATI LEARNED AN IMPORTANT LESSON ABOUT COOKING...
...AND SHE LEARNED HOW TO MAKE GOOD CURRY RICE.
WHAT'S UP WITH *THIS*?! EVEN YOUR *EGGS* TASTE LIKE CURRY!
BUT THAT'S ALL I KNOW HOW TO MAKE!

Kimika Aso
Kimika was Hitoshi's first love. Yet, try as he might, he could never get her to go out with him. It was out of pure desperation over this refusal that Hitoshi created Program #20. Though sometimes it seems that Kimika does not really *hate* Hitoshi, she really likes messing with him. If he had *really* tried, he might have gotten somewhere with her.

Program.10

The Lady Who Causes Storms

OH, MAN.
EVERY DAY IT DOES NOTHING BUT RAIN. I'M SICK OF IT.
HOW ABOUT YOU, SAATI?
PARADICE ARMY
EH? WHAT'S WRONG?
じ〜〜っ
ぱくっ
ゴーーー
OWWW!! HEY! QUIT IT!!
PARADICE ARMY
WHAT'S THE BIG IDEA, HUH?!
I'M SORRY. IT'S JUST...
...THERE WAS SOME DUST ON YOUR BREAD.
HUH?
SAATI, THAT'S MOLD!
JUST THROW IT AWAY!

MOLD?
YEAH. IT LOOKS LIKE DUST, BUT IT'S ACTUALLY A KIND OF PLANT.
YOU SEE IT A LOT DURING THE WET SEASON. IT'S WHERE THEY GET PENICILLIN FROM.
HMM. A KIND OF PLANT?
植物
DON'T WORRY, THOUGH. JUST THROW THAT BREAD AWAY.
I'LL GRAB SOME WHEN I HEAD OUT.
UGH, NOT AGAIN!
WHY'S IT ALWAYS HAFTA BE THIS WAY?
ALTHOUGH... IT WAS A RAINY DAY WHEN SAATI SHOWED UP.
WELCOME BACK...
IF IT WEREN'T FOR THAT STORM--
SO MAYBE I SHOULD BE THANKFUL.
WAAARGH!!

SAATI, I'M HOME!
ガチャ
JEEZ, IT'S *POURING* OUT THERE!
HITOSHI-SAN! COME QUICK! LOOK!
LOOK AT WHAT *I* GREW!
ジャーン
OH MY GOD!!
WHA- WHAT THE HELL?!
YOU *ARE* A *GIRL*, RIGHT?
ジョリ
ジョリジョリ
UM, I GUESS SO.
UH-OH! MY HAIR'S GROWING, TOO!
ぞわ
ぞわ
WHHAAA?!
ぞわ
ぞわ
ジョキ
ジョキ
ジョキ
WHAT THE HECK?!
IT JUST KEEPS GROWING BACK!

WHOA!
もわもわ
HUH? WHO TURNED OUT THE LIGHTS?
もわわ
OH MY GOD-- MY GIRLFRIEND'S A FURBALL!!

WHAT THE HELL IS GOING ON!
ずるずる
HITOSHI-SAN? IS THAT YOU?

WHA-WHAT THE HECK IS *THIS*?!
MY ROOM'S FULL OF MOLD!

IT LOOKS LIKE IT SNOWED IN HERE.
I KNOW IT'S THE RAINY SEASON, BUT THIS IS RIDICULOUS.

UM, ACTUALLY... THAT MOLD YOU SAW...

...I'VE KIND OF BEEN GROWING IT.

YOU'VE BEEN *WHAT?!*

PARADISE ARMY

GROWING *MOLD*, SILLY. THE DATABASE HAD ALL THE INFO. IT SAID MOLD GROWS WELL IN DARK AND DAMP AREAS.

▷MOLD
A MEMBER OF THE FU
PLANT KINGDOM. MOLD
THAT APPEARS ON THE S
PRODUCTS AND OTHER P

I FIGURED THAT SINCE YOUR ROOM IS THE DARKEST IN THE HOUSE...

...IT WOULD BE NICE TO HAVE A LOT OF FLOWERS AROUND!

MOLD DOESN'T HAVE FLOWERS! MOLD'S JUST... MOLD!

OH, GREAT. LOOK AT THIS.
EVEN THE *COMPUTER'S* COVERED IN MOLD.
I BET THAT MOLD'S RESPONSIBLE FOR YOUR HAIR PROBLEMS.
WE NEED TO GET THIS PLACE CLEANED UP
PARADISE ARMY

FIRST, WE BETTER DRY EVERYTHING WITH THE HAIR DRYER.
THEN WE'LL GET IT UP WITH THE VACUUM CLEANER.
HYPER DRY 1000
B-BUT IF YOU DO THAT, YOU'LL *KILL* IT ALL!
IF WE *DON'T* KILL ALL OF IT, IT'LL JUST GROW *BACK*!

POOR LITTLE GUYS. DIDN'T EVEN HAVE A CHANCE.
DO YOU KNOW HOW *UNHEALTHY* THIS IS?!

LISTEN, I'LL TAKE THE DEN! YOU TACKLE THIS ONE!
ALL RIGHT.

PHEW.
I THINK THAT'S ABOUT IT.

LOOKS LIKE MY HAIR IS BACK TO NORMAL TOO.

THE ONLY PLACE LEFT IS UNDER THE BED. EH, WHAT'S THIS?
A PHOTO ALBUM? IS IT HITOSHI'S?
Memory Album
AWWW, HOW CUTE!
HE USED TO BE SO LITTLE.
COULD THAT BE HIS LITTLE SISTER?
THEY LOOK LIKE THEY'RE HAVING SO MUCH FUN.
HAVING A BROTHER OR SISTER MUST BE NICE.
OH! THERE ARE SOME MORE UNDER HERE.
SUPPON-SUPER
580Yen
The Nude Centerfolds of 1993 Video Review Guide
The Hottest Babes For Your Pleasure

HMM. WHAT KIND OF BOOK...
...IS THIS?
WOW, THOSE ARE PRETTY BIG.

SAATI, I FINISHED UP IN--
OH MY GOD!
ARGH! D-DON'T LOOK AT THOSE!!
HITOSHI-SAN, WHAT KIND OF BOOK IS THAT?
UM... WELL, YOU SEE...

...IT'S, UM, IT'S A KIND OF REFERENCE BOOK. FOR, UH... PROGRAMMING.
I MEAN, IT'S NOT LIKE I USE IT FOR, UH... YOU KNOW.
I DON'T FOLLOW YOU.
OOPS.

HUH?
Danger! Do Not Touch!!
No. 20
IT'S A FLOPPY DISK.

NUMBER... 20?
WHAT'S ON THIS, HITOSHI-SAN?

DID YOU SAY...
...NUMBER 20?!

YEAH. SHOULD WE TAKE A LOOK?

NO!! ABSOLUTELY NOT! FORGET IT!!
PARADISE ARMY
IT'S *WAY* TOO DANGEROUS!

UM, I REALLY DON'T NEED THESE BOOKS ANYMORE. CAN YOU, UH, GO THROW THEM OUT?!
THAT COOL?!
UM, ARE YOU SURE YOU--
PARADISE ARMY

UH, THANKS A LOT!

NUMBER 20, HUH?
I HID THIS SO LONG AGO THAT I TOTALLY FORGOT WHERE IT WAS.
RMY

SO THIS IS THE ALPHA PROGRAM THAT I ORIGINALLY MADE?
THING TURNED OUT TO BE A TOTAL DISASTER.
Danger! Do Not Touch!!
No.20

THIS DISK IS FULL OF EMBARRASSING STUFF ABOUT ME.
I'VE GOTTA GET RID OF IT BEFORE SAATI FINDS IT.

BUT WHAT SHOULD I DO? I CAN'T JUST THROW IT AWAY.
I PUT TOO MUCH INTO THIS PROGRAM TO DO THAT!

BUT IF I LEAVE IT OUT, THEN SAATI MIGHT...

...I KNOW! I'LL JUST CONVERT THE DATA TO CODE AND SEAL IT UP.

THAT TAKES CARE OF THAT.

AHHHH!
WOW.
IT'S PRACTICALLY A TYPHOON OUT HERE.
I WONDER WHAT COULD BE ON THAT FLOPPY.
WHY IS IT NUMBERED LIKE I AM?
No.20
IT'S PRETTY BAD OUT THERE. I HOPE THE POWER DOESN'T GO OUT.
THEY'RE ALL GONE, HITOSHI-SAN.
BWAAGHHH!!

SO, WHAT ARE YOU DOING?
OH, UM, SINCE THE WEATHER'S SO BAD, I THOUGHT I SHOULD BACK THINGS UP.
YOU MEAN AS A BLACKOUT STRATEGY?
UH HUH.

THAT REMINDS ME, IS YOUR *OWN* BLACKOUT STRATEGY WORKING PROPERLY?
HUH?
I MEAN, HOW OFTEN DOES YOUR MEMORY AUTO-SAVE FUNCTION ACTIVATE?

IT'S SET ON A 60-MINUTE DEFAULT SYSTEM.

THAT WON'T DO. MY BACKUP POWER ONLY LASTS FOR ABOUT TEN MINUTES. YOU NEED TO SWITCH THAT.

PARADISE ARMY

BUT IF IT'S ONLY ONE HOUR'S WORTH OF NEW DATA...

...IT'S NOT THAT BIG OF A DEAL IF I LOSE IT, RIGHT?

WHAT ARE YOU TALKING ABOUT? WHAT ABOUT ALL THE STUFF THAT HAS HAPPENED IN THE PAST HOUR?

YOU REALLY WANT TO LOSE THAT?

YOU MIGHT NOT REALIZE THIS...
...BUT EVERY HOUR WE SPEND TOGETHER IS PRECIOUS.
......
OH, HITOSHI-SAN.
IT'S TRUE, SAATI.
AHH...
...AAHHCCHOOO!!
ぶっ
UHHH.
IS IT RAINING IN HERE?
SAATI, WHY DON'T YOU TAKE A BATH?
PPPP

チャポッ
HE SAID, "EVERY HOUR WE SPEND TOGETHER IS PRECIOUS."
HMMM.
ピチャッ
DO MY BREASTS NEED TO BE BIGGER? I DON'T KNOW.
I'M NOT SURE WHAT GUYS ARE LOOKING FOR.
WHAT HAPPENS IF A GIRL WHO'S MORE ATTRACTIVE THAN ME SHOWS UP?
WOULD HITOSHI-SAN WANT TO BE WITH HER INSTEAD?

PERFECT! NOW'S MY CHANCE.
THIS SHOULD GIVE ME JUST ENOUGH TIME TO SEAL UP THAT DISK.
カチッ
FIRST, WE THE COMPRESS THE DATA...
...AND THEN WE CONVERT IT INTO RAW CODE.
GOOD, EASIER THAN I THOUGHT.
WELL, THIS SHOULD TAKE ABOUT 20 MINUTES.
ヴーン
ゴオオオ
ギシ
ギシ
ギシ
ギシ
ARGH!!
ゴウアアアア

DAMMIT!!
A BLACKOUT?!
SAATI, ARE YOU OKAY?
UH, YEAH.
SO, THIS IS A BLACK-OUT, HUH?
Emergency Generator
WAIT...
...OH CRAP! THE DISK!!

en cancelled.
blip

CRAP! IT STOPPED HALF-WAY THROUGH!!
DANG IT! NOW I'VE GOTTA DO IT ALL OVER AGAIN.

WHA--?!
PARADISE ARM

NO!! YOU CAN'T *DO* THIS TO ME!!

I'VE GOTTA SHUT IT DOWN BEFORE--

BAARGH!!!
WARGGH

ボウン
OH SHIT!!
モクモク…
BLEEP
Program No. 20
NO. 20 HAS STOPPED RESPONDING
Program No. 20
ヌヌッ
ヌ〜〜ッ
EH HEH.

UMMPH!!
HI-HITOSHI-SAN?!
OH MY GOSH!!
WHAT IS ALL THIS?!
WAARPHH!!
YOU CALLED AND I CAME FLYING OUT.
TA-DAH!!

MY, IT HAS BEEN QUITE A WHILE, HASN'T IT?
NICE TO SEE YOU'VE GROWN, HITOSHI-KUN.
TW-TWENTY?!
"HITOSHI-KUN?!" WHO THE HELL IS SHE?

KEN AKAMATSU TELLS ALL

Musings from Ken Akamatsu about what he does in his spare time and the movies he likes!!

Tell us, what do you do in your spare time?

Akamatsu: Hmmm. I guess I'd have to say working on my web site and playing online games. Working on my web site is fun whenever I have some free time, but my favorite computer games are **Ultima** and **Diablo.**

That's kind of a weird way to relax isn't it?

Akamatsu: Yeah, I guess it is. Actually though, I've been so busy recently that the only real recreation I have time for anymore is checking my e-mail and updating my blog.

Sometimes I only have about 5 seconds to write something.

Sometimes I only have about 5 seconds to write something. So, I end up only posting, like, one line. (laughs)

Well, if you did have more free time, what would you like to do?

Akamatsu: I've got this stack of videos that I've been meaning to watch. I got **Independence Day** the other day, and I keep wondering when **Godzilla** is finally going to come out on video, because I really like Roland Emmerich's* work.

Now that we're on the subject of movies, what kind of movies do you like?

I liked **Romancing the Stone**, but everything he does be it drama, comedy or whatever, is all pretty good. If Spielberg would back off a little, I'm sure Zemeckis** would be on top.

So, I end up only posting, like, one line.

What about before you went to college?

Akamatsu: In high school I watched a lot of old, live-action "stop motion animation" stuff. I liked anything by Ray Harryhausen,*** and I watched **The 7th Voyage of Sinbad** over and over again. Harryhausen was the apprentice of the guy who made **King Kong,** and his most brilliant "stop motion" work was making skeletons move. It looked like 8mm film footage.

* The German-born director known for his work on Independence Day, Stargate and The Patriot.
** The director who became best known for the Back to the Future trilogy and Forrest Gump.
*** A special effects guru who is famous for using "stop motion animation."

Continued on Page 114

A.I.
LOVE YOU
Program.11
She's a Real Hottie!

SO, TELL ME, HITOSHI-KUN.
DID YOU MISS ME?
N-NUMBER TWENTY?! YOU'RE HERE?!
NUMBER TWENTY?!
THE LAST TIME YOU HAD YOUR WAY WITH ME WAS JULY 14TH, RIGHT?

OWWW! LET GO OF MY HAIR!! STOP!!
WHAT THE HELL ARE YOU DOING?!
PLEASE, MISS TWENTY, GO BACK WHERE YOU CAME FROM!!
GO BACK? NOW THAT'S NOT RIGHT.
WE HAVEN'T SEEN EACH OTHER IN FOREVER AND THIS IS HOW YOU ACT?
UH...
...WELL, I--
HITOSHI-SAN, JUST WHO IS THIS?
WELL, Y-YOU SEE, UM--
HUSH, DEAR. I CAN RECAP.

YOU MEAN SHE'S MY BIG *SISTER?!*

WHY DIDN'T YOU INTRODUCE US EARLIER?!

UM, WELL, THERE'S A REASON.

* A programming language that uses human-readable text which is later turned into binary code via an assembler. Assembly Language's biggest asset is that it is very speed-efficient.

I MADE HER BECAUSE I WAS DEPRESSED, BUT SHE MADE IT WORSE.
WHAT?! YOU GOT TURNED DOWN AGAIN?!
IT'S 'CAUSE YOU'RE ALWAYS WHACKING OFF.
WITH HER, IT WAS ALWAYS ABOUT HAVING A GOOD TIME. MAYBE, IT'S MY FAULT FOR DESIGNING HER TOO PERFECTLY.
BUT SOMEHOW, SHE GREW INTO THIS NAGGING BEAUTY QUEEN.
HOW'S MY HAIR? IT LOOK OKAY? WAIT, IS THAT A FRECKLE?!
DOES THIS DRESS MAKE ME LOOK FAT?
PARADISE ARMY

AFTER A WHILE, I JUST COULDN'T TAKE IT ANYMORE AND STOPPED RUNNING HER.
YEAH. WHATEVER, HITOSHI-KUN.
NOW, WHO THE HELL IS SHE?

UM, THIS IS SAATI. SHE'S A PROGRAM JUST LIKE YOU.
EXCEPT SHE WAS MADE IN C.
PARADISE ARMY

HMMMM.

THE REASON HE HASN'T TOUCHED ME IN A YEAR IS BECAUSE HE MADE HER?!
IT'S NICE TO MEET YOU, SIS.
I'VE ALWAYS WANTED TO HAVE A SISTER... AND NOW YOU'RE HERE!

DID YOU JUST CALL ME "SIS"?!
MY, *YOU'RE* AWFULLY FRIENDLY, AREN'T YOU?
AAAHHH!!
WAAGHH?!
WHAT THE HECK ARE YOU--
WELL, WELL, WELL.
HEIGHT: 166CM.
WEIGHT: 44KG.
BUST: 82CM.
WAIST: 58.
HIPS: 85.

HOW CAN THIS PITIFUL THING BE MY SISTER?
YOU'RE MEAN!
I'M SORRY, BUT YOU ARE SORELY LACKING.
NOW WATCH AND LEARN, GIRL!!
OBSEVE MY VOLUPTUOUS BUST!
ばんっ
THIS 86CM RACK IS THAT OF SUPER-MODEL REIKO KATOO!
I HAVE AI IIJIMA TO THANK FOR MY TIGHT LITTLE 88CM ASS!
どんっ
AND...
...MY UNBEATABLY SMOOTH, LONG LEGS COME FROM CHISATO MORITAKA!
びしっ
I'M SORRY, BUT YOUR HOMELY LITTLE OFFERINGS...
...CAN'T EVEN COMPARE TO MY PERFECT BODY!!
MY SISTER'S REALLY WEIRD.
.....

LOOK, WE GET IT ALREADY. YOU'RE PERFECT!
NOW, WHY DON'T YOU JUST GO ON BACK?

....
NO WAY, JOSÉ.

I FINALLY MADE IT INTO THE REAL WORLD. AND I AIN'T GOING BACK.
I'M GONNA STAY RIGHT HERE AND PARTY MY ASS OFF!

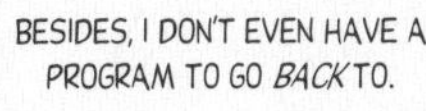
BESIDES, I DON'T EVEN HAVE A PROGRAM TO GO *BACK* TO.

WHAT?!

AND I KNOW YOU'D *LOVE* TO HAVE A HOT CHICK LIKE *ME* LIVING HERE.
UH, NO I WOULDN'T!!
PARADISE

WHO SAID YOU COULD *LIVE* HERE?
I THOUGHT THAT WAS A GIVEN.
GIVEN?!

IF YOU DON'T SHUT THE HELL UP...
...I'M GONNA TELL HER ALL ABOUT THOSE PORNO VIDEOS UNDER YOUR DESK...*AND* ABOUT THOSE *CONVERSATIONS* WE USED TO HAVE!

YOU...YOU WOULDN'T!!
WHAT DO I DO NOW?!
THIS'LL BE GREAT, SIS.
HMPH.
THERE'S NO WAY WE CAN ALL LIVE TOGETHER.
STOP FOLLOWING ME.

UGGHH...
...WHAT AM I SUPPOSED TO DO NOW?

ポタッ
OKAY, TIME OUT.

THIS PLACE GOT SERIOUSLY WRECKED. JUST LOOK AT THE CEILING.
LET'S SORT THIS OUT AFTER WE GET THE LEAKS FIXED.
DON'T WORRY, HITOSHI-SAN.
JUST LEAVE IT TO ME.
OH, YOU HAVE AN IDEA?
YEP.
INITIATING STRUCTURE SCAN.
SCAN: COMPLETE. 581 KNOWN LEAKS PRESENT.
PARADISE ARMY
MY SCAN INDICATES THERE ARE 581 LEAKS.
SO, FIRST, DRINK THESE, OKAY?
AND THEN WHAT?
ISN'T IT OBVIOUS? WE'LL USE THE EMPTY CANS TO CATCH THE WATER!
HOW AM I GONNA DRINK THAT MUCH SODA, HUH?!

AHH, I CAN'T EVEN STAND TO WATCH THIS.
WE HAVE TO DO SOMETHING ABOUT THE WATER, RIGHT?
HERE, ALLOW ME.
GO FOR IT, SIS!
THIS IS MAKING ME EVEN MORE NERVOUS.
PROGRAM OPTION NUMBER TWO!
ACCELERATION: MAXIMUM POWER!!
HERE I GO!!
VZT!
ビリ
ビリッ
LIKE MY OUTFIT?

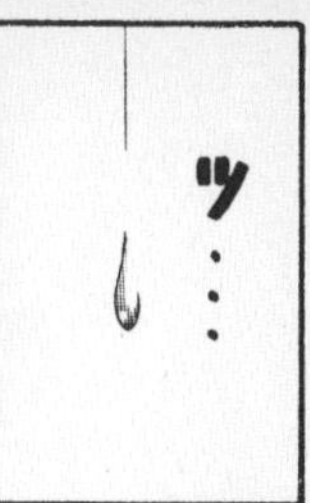
ツ…

フワッ…

WHOA!!
フワ フワ..
PARADISE ARM

JEEZ, TWENTY!
I DIDN'T KNOW YOU HAD THAT MUCH *POWER!*
PARADISE A

I'M MORE THAN JUST GOOD LOOKS, AFTER ALL.

I'M FAST, EFFICIENT AND POWERFUL. SO, HOW 'BOUT IT?
CAN YOU DO ANYTHING LIKE THAT WITH YOUR LOW LEVEL A.I.?

NOPE!
WOW, SIS! YOU'RE AMAZING!

AH, YOU AGREE WITH ME THEN! IT'S SETTLED! I AM THE BEST!!
AH HA HA HA HA!!

UM, HOW'D YOU GET THE WATER TO FLOAT IN MID-AIR?
AH, HITOSHI-KUN. CAN'T YOU GUESS?
PARADISE ARMY

I SIMPLY INFUSED THE WATER MOLECULES WITH ELECTRICITY.
THEY'RE FLOATING BECAUSE OF THE ION-WIND EFFECT.*
H2O

DID SHE SAY...
...ELECTRICITY?!
PARADISE ARMY
W-WHAT IF YOU TOUCH ONE?
WELL, DUH. YOU FREAKIN' DIE.

* A theory that equates high voltage with anti-gravity. Some researchers use this theory to explain how UFOs are able to fly.

H-HEY--GET THEM OUTTA HERE, THEN!
HUSH! IF WE GET ALL THE DROPS IN ONE PLACE, WE CAN GET RID OF THEM ALL AT ONCE.
OKAY, WE'LL PUT THEM IN THE BATHROOM.
SOUNDS GOOD.
THAT'S ALL OF THEM.
WE HAD THAT MUCH WATER LEAKING IN?!
HMMM.
I THINK I SEE WHERE THIS IS GOING.
PARADISE ARMY
SO YOU'RE GOING TO CUT THE VOLTAGE AND JUST LET IT DRAIN?
THAT'S RIGHT. EH?
HUH? WHAT'S THAT?

ポロッ
AWRIGHTY, LETS DO IT.
ポトッ
......
HUH? IS SOMETHING WRONG?
AAAH!
EEECCCCKKK!!!
A BUG! THERE'S A BUG!
A BUG? WHERE?!
NO! GET AWAY FROM ME!!
ドン
WAARGH!!

HANG IN THERE! I'M... KYYAAAAHHH!!
THE VOLTAGE IS TOO STRONG!
I DON'T KNOW HOW SHE DID IT, BUT THERE'S A WALL OF ELECTRICITY KEEPING HIM IN.
AND NOW FOR A TIME OUT.
IF YOU HAVE NOT GUESSED BY NOW, THE REASON TWENTY TOTALLY SPAZZED OUT OVER A COCKROACH IS DUE TO THE FACT SHE CAN'T DIFFERENTIATE BETWEEN A COMPUTER 'BUG' AND THE CREEPY-CRAWLY INSECT VARIETY.
PARADISE ARMY
SIS...SIS? PLEASE, YOU HAVE TO DO SOMETHING!
きゅ～
OH NO, SHE'S LOCKED UP! WHAT SHOULD I DO NOW?!
HITOSHI-SAN DOESN'T HAVE MUCH LONGER!
ゴボ
ゴボ
ゴボ
GLUG GLAAH!
PARADISE ARMY
I KNOW! IF I EXERT MORE OUTPUT THAN HER...
...THE ELECTRIC SHIELD MIGHT BREAK DOWN.

PROGRAM OPTION NUMBER TWO!
MAXIMUM ACCELERATION!
ガボ
PLEASE, HITOSHI-SAN! DON'T DIE!!
UGH, NO GOOD.
THERE'S STILL NOT ENOUGH OUTPUT.
YOU'VE GOT TO STAY STRONG, SAAT!!
JUST STAY STRONG!!
PARADISE

ゴボ
ゴボゴボ
HITOSHI-SAN!

バシャッ
ゴン

HITOSHI-SAN! WAKE UP!
ピューーッ

No.20
Resumed ru
HAAH?!
HUH?
HEY, ARE WE ALL FINISHED TALKING?
I WONDER WHERE THOSE TWO WENT.
AH!
IS EVERYTHING OKAY NOW?
YEAH, I'M FINE.
GOOD TO HEAR. I WAS REALLY WORRIED.
HEH HEH. SORRY FOR THE TROUBLE.

WHAT? THEY LEFT ME BY MYSELF...

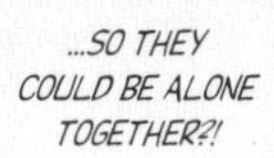

...SO THEY COULD BE ALONE TOGETHER?!

THAT'S IT!

I'M NOT GONNA STOP...

...UNTIL HITOSHI IS MINE.

メラメラ

メラ

HUH?

SOMEBODY GET THE RAID!!

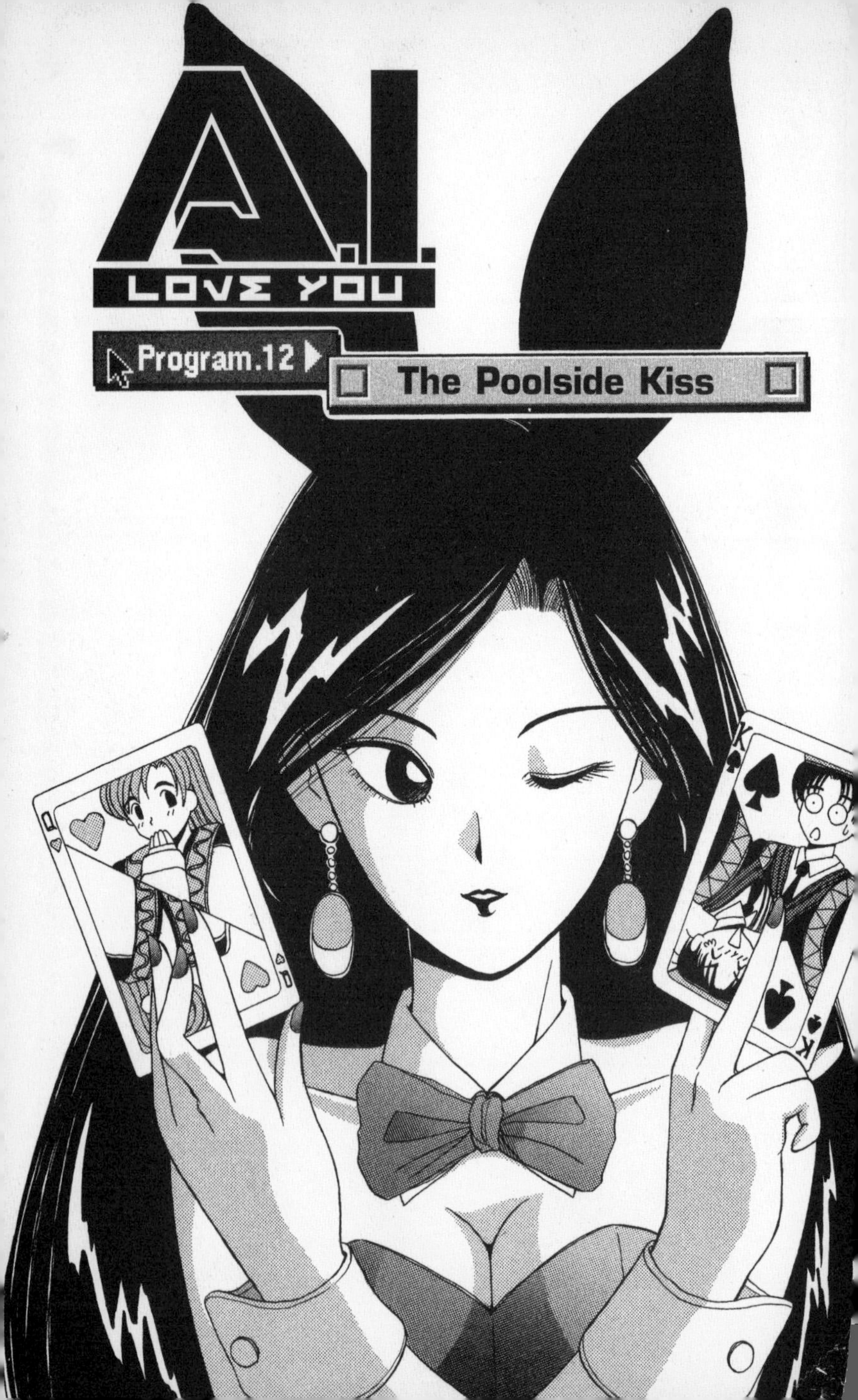
A.I. LOVE YOU
Program.12
The Poolside Kiss

OKAY, OKAY.
WHOA!
OH, CRAP! NOT MY COMPUTER!
ゴボゴボ
HUH?
IS THE COMPUTER YOU DROPPED AN OLD 286?
OR IS IT THIS BRAND NEW PENTIUM?
ACTUALLY, IT'S THE OLD 286, BUT--
THE...THE PENTIUM.
LIAR!!

バシャーン
AAAHH!
ドン
ゴボ
GULB BLUUB!!
ゴボ
ゴボ
HELP ME! I DON'T WANNA DIE!!
ぐっ
がばっ
HAAAH!!
PHEW. JUST A DREAM.
HMM?
むにゅ
HUWAAAHHHHH!
UUUUZZZZ.
HUH, WHAT ARE YOU YELLIN' ABOUT?
サッ
TWENTY! WHAT ARE YOU DOING IN HERE?! AND YOU'RE... YOU'RE...NAKED!!

GOOD MORNING, HITOSHI-SAN!
IT'S 7 O'CLOCK, SLEEPY HEAD.
KYAA!
UH--
S-SIS...
...Y-YOU'RE NAKED.
NO, SAATI! IT'S NOT WHAT IT LOOKS LIKE!!
WHERE ELSE WAS I SUPPOSED TO SLEEP? NO ROOM, REMEMBER?
WE DIDN'T! I WOULDN'T!! SHE'S ONLY NAKED BECAUSE--
GOD, DO YOU EVER SHUT UP?!
THIS ISN'T THE BATH, SILLY. THAT'S UPSTAIRS.
THAT'S WHERE YOU CAN GET NAKED.
I KNEW IT!
I DIDN'T JUST DREAM IT! ALL THAT CRAP WAS REAL!

HOW IN THE WORLD CAN THESE THREE...
THE SUPER DITZ
THE SUPER HOTTIE
...POSSIBLY LIVE TOGETHER PEACEFULLY?

IF YOU DON'T HURRY UP, YOU'LL BE LATE!
YEAH, YOU'RE RIGHT.

WHERE ARE YOU GOING SO EARLY IN THE MORNING?

UH, WHERE ELSE... SCHOOL.
YOU FORGET ALREADY?

WAIT, DIDN'T YOU TELL ME YOU *HATED* SCHOOL?

UH, MAYBE!

YOU USED TO ALWAYS COME CRYING TO ME ABOUT HOW MUCH YOU SUCKED AT SP ORTS AND HOW NO GIRLS EVER LIKED YOU.

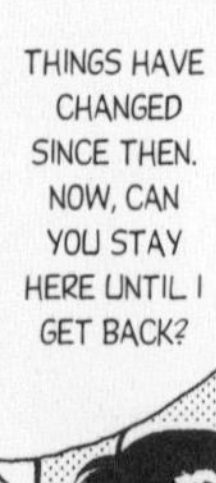
THINGS HAVE CHANGED SINCE THEN. NOW, CAN YOU STAY HERE UNTIL I GET BACK?

YOU READY, SAATI?
SURE AM.

HMMPH!
WHAT'S SHE SO HAPPY ABOUT, HUH?

SHE BETTER LAUGH IT UP WHILE SHE CAN...
...BECAUSE AS SOON AS HITOSHI RECOGNIZES MY SUPERIORITY, HE'LL BE MINE HANDS DOWN.

キーン
コーン

OH, THAT'S RIGHT. TODAY'S THE "POOL OPENING."
Todays P.E. Class Swim

UGH, THIS COULD SUCK.
HMM. A POOL OPENING?

YOU MEAN THE POOL'S GOING TO CRACK OPEN...

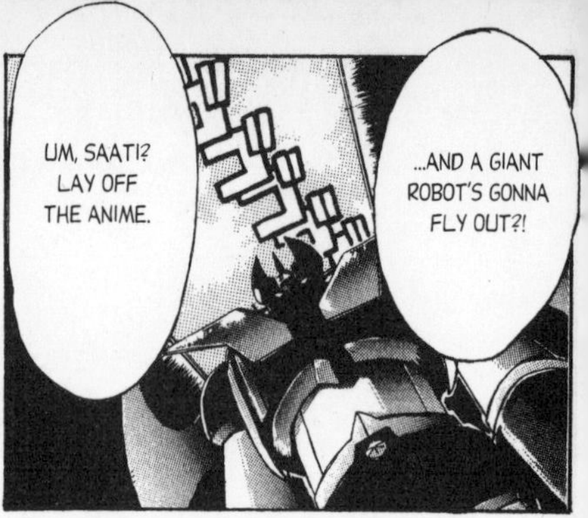
...AND A GIANT ROBOT'S GONNA FLY OUT?!
UM, SAATI? LAY OFF THE ANIME.

OR MAYBE THERE'S A PATRIOT MISSILE HIDDEN INSIDE!
OKAY, YOU'RE DEFINITELY OUT IN LEFT FIELD THERE.

LOOK, TODAY'S THE FIRST DAY WE GET TO GO SWIMMING.
IT'S KINDA SPECIAL, SO WE GET TO BE CO-ED TODAY.
THAT SOUNDS SORTA FUN... I GUESS.

IT'S NOT. IT'S TORTURE.
はあ…
AND HERE I AM, MR. CAN'T-SWIM-WORTH-A-FLIP.
THAT'S OKAY. WE CAN PRACTICE TOGETHER.
Locker r

ザワ ザワ ザワ

HUH? WHAT'S ALL THE COMMOTION ABOUT?

WHAAAA--?!

T-TWENTY? WHAT IS SHE DOIN' HERE?!

NOW, NOW, HITOSHI. IT'S *TONI.*

BESIDES, YOU'RE LATE. NOW, HURRY UP. I WANNA GO SWIMMING.

AH!
SIS, IS THAT YOU?!
WHEN'D YOU GET HERE?!
DID SHE SAY "SIS?!"
YEAH, THAT'S RIGHT. SHE'S SAATI'S BIG SISTER.
SHE JUST MOVED OUT HERE AND NOW SHE'S LIVING WITH US.
HI THERE. I'M TONI.
HONESTLY, I JUST CAME TO CHECK OUT THE CLASS TODAY.
I KNOW HITOSHI'S PRETTY PATHETIC, BUT DON'T PICK ON HIM, 'KAY?
YES, MA'AM!!

WOW, SIS! I LOVE YOUR SWIMSUIT.
DIDN'T I TELL YOU TO STOP FOLLOWING ME AROUND?
AFTER THAT, HOW COULD WE NOT PICK ON YOU?!
BUT YOU SAID--
YOU'RE JUST BEGGING FOR A BEATING, AREN'T YA?!
ボコ
ボコ
ボコ
QUIT FOOLIN' AROUND OR YOU'RE GONNA BE RUNNIN' LAPS!!
AND... YOU ARE?
ニコッ
ME? WHY, JUST ONE OF HITOSHI'S RELATIVES.
ACTUALLY, I'VE BEEN WORRIED ABOUT HITOSHI'S GRADES.
IF YOU DON'T MIND, I'D LOVE TO SIT AND WATCH.
すりすり
THAT'S NOT A PROBLEM, IS IT?
• • •
UH, WELL, I GUESS THAT'S OKAY.
ALL RIGHT, TIME TO WARM UP!!
DO IT OR YOU'LL DROWN!!
GOD...THIS SUCKS.
HITOSHI-KUN!
HUH?

BE A DEAR AND LOTION MY BACK, PLEASE.
ARGH! CAN'T YOU DO IT YOURSELF?!
I'M GETTING CREAMED OUT HERE 'CAUSE OF YOU!!
AWWW, YOU KNOW YOU WANNA.
ME? UH, NO. I--
THERE'S NO WAY HE COULD LOOK AT MY BODY WITHOUT FEELING SOME-THING DOWN THERE.
OH REALLY?
YOU MIGHT...
...NEVER GET A CHANCE LIKE THIS AGAIN.
ドキ
ドキ
ドキ
ALL RIGHT, FINE.
BUT JUST A LITTLE.

MY SEDUCTION STRATEGY IS WORKING PERFECTLY.
ぬりッ
ぬりッ ぬりッ

HE'S RIGHT WHERE I WANT HIM.
ニヤッ

OH MY GOD!
ぬり ぬり
ぬり
THIS IS TOO GOOD TO BE TRUE.

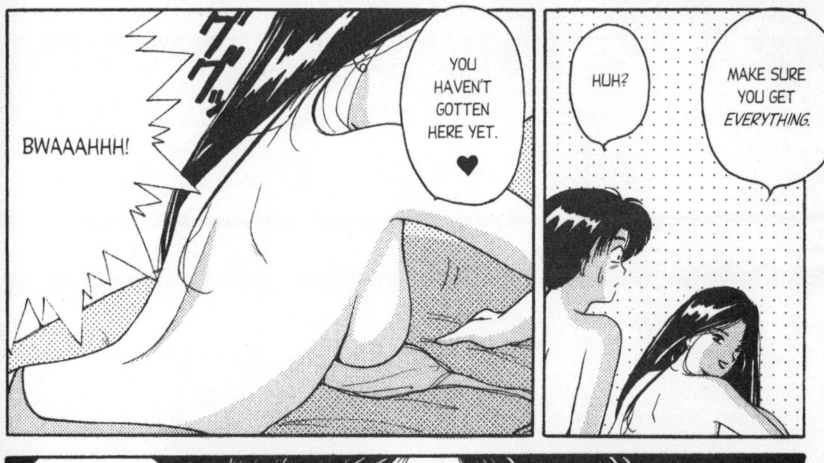
MAKE SURE YOU GET EVERYTHING.
HUH?
YOU HAVEN'T GOTTEN HERE YET. ♥
BWAAAHHH!

HITOSHI... SWEETIE.
...DON'T YOU WANT ME ALL TO YOURSELF?

I'M *WAY* MORE ATTRACTIVE THAN THAT OTHER GIRL, AREN'T I?
OH, HOW I WISH YOU WERE IN LOVE WITH ME.
WHY DON'T YOU TOUCH ME AND SEE WHAT IT'S LIKE? ♥
OOOH, THAT'S RIGHT, HITOSHI.
MMM... YOU'RE PRETTY GOOD.
スリスリ
OKAY, SIS. THE OIL'S ALL RUBBED IN.
AAAAAHHHHH!!
IT'S YOU!!
WHY THE HELL ARE *YOU* RUBBING OIL ON ME?!
HUH? BUT HITOSHI-SAN SAID--
WITH A PAINT BRUSH, NO LESS!!!
きゅ〜〜

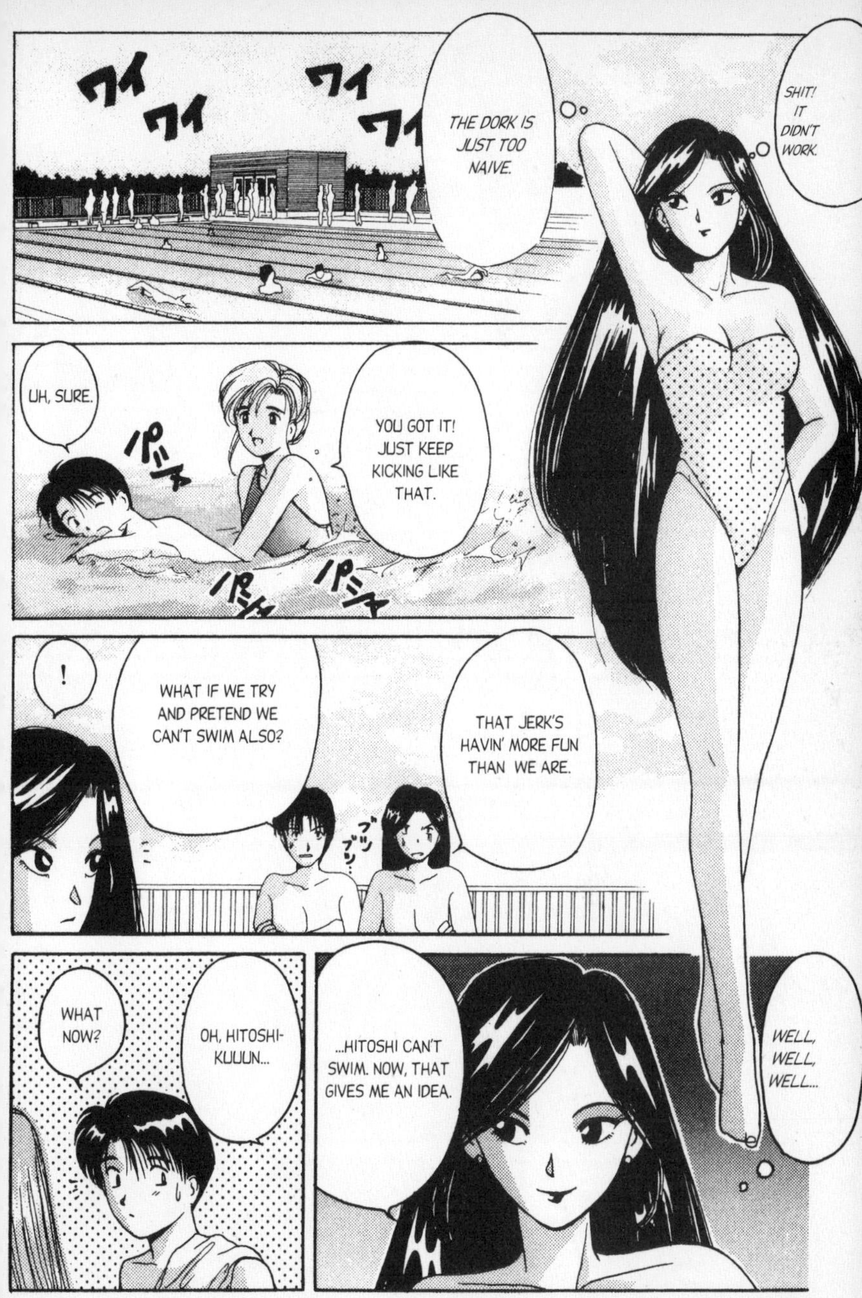

SHIT! IT DIDN'T WORK.
THE DORK IS JUST TOO NAIVE.
ワイワイ
ワイワイ
YOU GOT IT! JUST KEEP KICKING LIKE THAT.
UH, SURE.
パシャ
パシャ
THAT JERK'S HAVIN' MORE FUN THAN WE ARE.
ブツブツ…
WHAT IF WE TRY AND PRETEND WE CAN'T SWIM ALSO?
!
WELL, WELL, WELL...
...HITOSHI CAN'T SWIM. NOW, THAT GIVES ME AN IDEA.
OH, HITOSHI-KUUUN...
WHAT NOW?

I HEAR YOU CAN'T SWIM. I CAN FIX THAT FOR YOU.
NAH, THAT'S OKAY.
IT'S NO TROUBLE. IN FACT, I CAN TURN YOU INTO A PRO RIGHT NOW.
WOW, SIS! CAN YOU REALLY DO THAT?
JEEZ, I WONDER IF THIS'LL REALLY WORK.
I HOPE YOU'RE READY FOR IT, MY DEAR!
IF I CAN MAKE HIM SWIM, HE'LL HAVE NO CHOICE BUT FALL FOR ME.
パリ
パリ
パリ
パリ
PROGRAM OPTION NUMBER EIGHT! MAXIMUM POWER!!
WATER ELEMENTALS, HEED MY COMMAND! COME CRASHING DOWN!!
AAAAAAHHHHHHH!!

ザッパー

GURGLE GURGABLE...!
GLUB...!

OH MY! HITOSHI'S SWIMMING SO FAST!
I WOULDN'T CALL THAT *SWIMMING!*

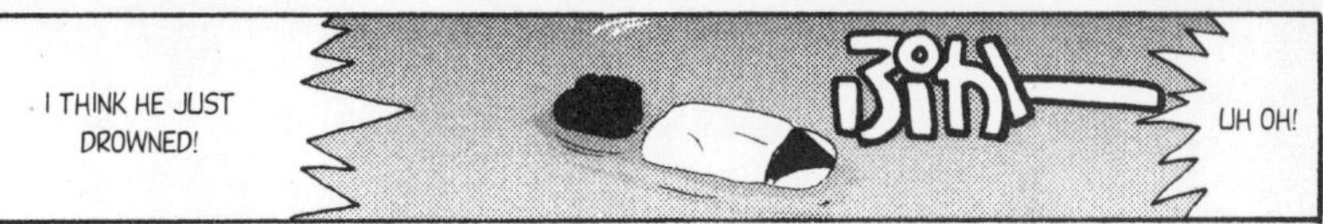
UH OH!
ぷかー
I THINK HE JUST DROWNED!

JUST GO FREAKIN' HOME ALREADY!!
I COULD HAVE *DIED* BACK THERE!!
UM, OOPSIE?

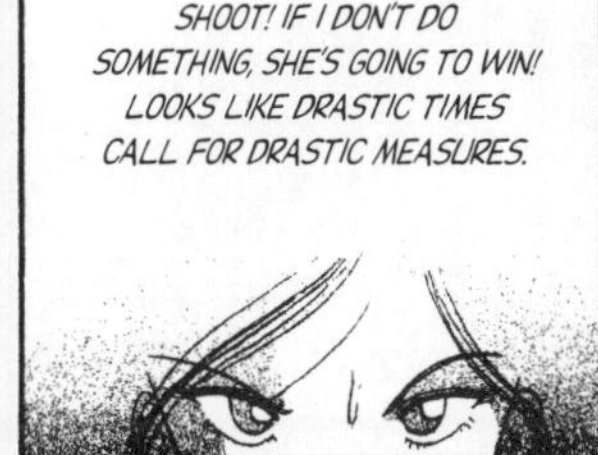
SHOOT! IF I DON'T DO SOMETHING, SHE'S GOING TO WIN! LOOKS LIKE DRASTIC TIMES CALL FOR DRASTIC MEASURES.

SEE, IT WAS HORRIBLE.
ARE YOU OKAY?

HUH?
WHAT THE--?!

OH, HELP! I'M... DROWNING!!
PLEASE! SAVE ME, HITOSHI!!
バシャ
バシャ
バシャ

T-TONI?!
OH DEAR! SIS!!

HITOSHI'S SO KIND-HEARTED.
バシャ
バシャ
ALL I HAVE TO DO IS PRETEND I'M DROWNING AND HE'LL COME RUNNING.

THEN, HE'LL GIVE ME MOUTH TO MOUTH...
...AND THAT'LL BE IT. HE'LL BE ALL MINE.

WHAT SHOULD I DO?
SHE'S GOING TO DROWN IF I DON'T HELP HER!

HANG ON, SIS!
バッ
I'LL SAVE YOU!!
ALL RIGHT, SAATI!
NO, DAMMIT! I DON'T NEED HER TO SAVE ME!!
ブク
ブク

AHHH!
W-WHAT'S HAPPENING?
MY LEG... IT JUST CRAMPED UP.
KYAAAAAHH!
AHHH! HELP ME.
OH NO! SAATI-SAN'S IN
IT LOOKS LIKE A CRAMP!!
SAATI!!

WHAT?!
I'M COMING!!
HANG ON, SAATI!!
ビチャ
バチャ
バチャ
バチャ
WHOAAAA!
HITOSHI'S ACTUALLY SWIMMING!
HITOSHI-SAN!
EASY, NOW! I'VE GOT YOU!!
ワー
HI-HITOSHI-SAN?
ワー
ワー
JUST GRAB ONTO ME!
HUH? MY FEET ARE ON THE BOTTOM.

HOW'S YOUR LEG?
DOES IT HURT ANY?
I'LL BE OKAY. THANKS, HITOSHI-SAN.
AH, GOOD.
HEY, HITOSHI!
WHY DIDN'T YOU JUMP IN WHEN I WAS DROWNING?
YOU DIDN'T EVEN HESITATE WHEN IT WAS HER!
UM, WELL--
I JUST DON'T GET IT.
YOU LIKE THIS AIR-HEADED DITZ MORE THAN ME?
I WASN'T GOING TO BRING THIS UP, BUT...

BUT...

...THAT WAS--

G-GIRL-FRIEND?

TELL ME...

...WAS THAT JUST A LIE?

Did you ever attempt to make your own films?

Akamatsu: Yes, I made a couple while I was in college. I made some action flicks, some anime and a few romantic comedies. And, obviously, I tried to use beautiful young girls in those. (laughs)

Then you were more interested in filmmaking than in illustrating at first?

Akamatsu: Absolutely, but I still get to deal with the film aspect a bit in my current field. I used to work with 8mm film, so I always have something to talk about with animators. All animation companies use the same "stop motion" techniques that live action films do. For instance, with animation you have to carefully draw a picture for each tiny movement. With manga, even though I'm doing still drawings, I try to create movement in each panel. If you look at the cover illustrations for this volume and the last one, it almost seems as if the characters are actually in the ocean and moving with the current of the sea.

I liked reading it...

Was that feeling of movement influenced by your old animation techniques?

Akamatsu: Maybe. I started as an animator, and since animation is a moving picture, if you don't draw several angles you can't get that sense of movement. In that regard, I think my experience as an animator has helped me a lot as an illustrator.

Did you have any interest in manga at the time?

Akamatsu: No, actually, I didn't. I liked reading it, but I thought it was too much trouble to draw.

Really? But you're quite good considering that you didn't start drawing manga until after college.

Akamatsu: I did a lot of training in a short period of time. I was in the anime club and the manga club, but the anime club was more popular at my college. There were even professors in our club. So, I was sort of trained that way.

...but I thought it was too much trouble to draw.

Now you sometimes use your P.C. to do illustrations, correct?

Akamatsu: The great thing about illustrating with a computer is that you can keep making as many changes as you want. If you mess up with a paintbrush, then that's it. Also, with a P.C. you can make several versions of each drawing. So, if you don't think the sky isn't quite right, you can change the color with the click of a button.

Continued on page 136

KEN AKAMATSU Special talk

THE WORLD OF A.I. LOVE YOU

LOVE TALK!

KEN AKAMATSU TELLS ALL

Musings from Ken Akamatsu about his past, drawing techniques, and college films!!

A.I.
LOVE YOU
Program.13
Love Triangle

WHAT DO YOU MEAN, "GIRLFRIEND"?

YOU HEARD ME.
A LONG TIME AGO, HITOSHI ASKED ME TO BE HIS GIRLFRIEND.

W-WHAT?

W-W-WAIT A SEC! THAT'S NOT--
WRAAGH!!
ぐいっ

HITOSHI AND I ARE LOVERS!
SO, WHY DON'T YOU STOP TRYING TO GET IN OUR WAY?!

RIGHT...
...LOVE MUFFIN?
CHU
W-WAIT, SAATI!!
WHAT WAS THAT?
IT'S NOT TRUE! SHE'S LYING!!
HEH HEH! NOW THAT SHE'S OUT OF THE PICTURE...
...HITOSHI IS ALL MINE FOR THE TAKING!
YOU CHEAT-ING LITTLE PUNK!
ARGH! HELP!!
YOU'RE DEAD!!

DID HITOSHI REALLY ASK SIS TO BE HIS GIRLFRIEND TOO?

UNNH.

THAT IF I BECOME A REAL GIRL...
...YOU WOULD LET ME BE YOUR GIRL-FRIEND?

BUT...WHAT DID HE MEAN WHEN HE SAID THAT TO ME?
THERE MUST HAVE BEEN A PROGRAMMING ERROR. IT'S THE ONLY EXPLANATION.

BUT WHY...
...WHY DO I HAVE THIS STRANGE FEELING?

MAYBE HITOSHI-SAN ONLY WANTS A GIRL WHO LOOKS LIKE THIS.

!

IF I GET A BODY LIKE THAT TOO...
...WOULD HITOSHI-SAN NOTICE ME THEN?

THAT'S IT!

Huge Bargain

IT'S GETTING PRETTY LATE.
AND SAATI'S NOT BACK YET.

I STILL CAN'T BELIEVE...
...THAT YOU ACTUALLY SAID THAT!

BUT IT IS TRUE.
YOU DID ASK ME TO BE YOUR GIRLFRIEND.

BUT YOU--
I'M HOME!

SAATI?
AH, GOOD. YOU'RE BACK!
バタバタバタ

WHERE'D YOU GO?!
WE'VE BEEN WOR-RIED.

I'M BACK, HITOSHI-SAN.
UWAAHHHH!!
SAATI, IS THAT YOU?!
HOW DO YOU LIKE MY NEW OUTFIT?
すりすり
AH, HEH HEH!
B-BR-BRE--
YOUR HEART'S BEATING SO FAST...
...IS SOMETHING WRONG?
SAATI...
バッ
...WHAT HAS GOTTEN INTO YOU?!
THAT LOOK'S NOT YOU!

BUT...
...BUT I THOUGHT YOU LIKED THIS KIND OF LOOK.
......
WELL, YOU'RE WRONG, SAATI.
WHEN HAVE I EVER ASKED YOU TO DRESS LIKE THAT?!
YOU LOOK LIKE A SLUT IN THAT!
I...I--
HUH?

I'M SORRY THAT MY LOOK DOESN'T PLEASE YOU ANYMORE!
I KNOW I WON'T EVER BE ABLE TO LOOK AS SEXY AS TONI DOES! I GOT THAT!
WAIT, SAATI...
...DON'T OVERREACT.
HITOSHI-SAN!
YOU'RE A JERK!!

OOMPH!
カッ
パアアッ
SAATI?!
WHAT ARE YOU DOING?!
イイィ...
AWW, DAMN.
YOU MADE HER ANGRY.
HUH?
YOU REALLY DON'T UNDER-STAND GIRLS AT ALL, DO YOU?
NO WONDER SHE'S MAD AT YOU.

SHE WORE THAT CRAP BECAUSE SHE THOUGHT IT'D MAKE YOU LIKE HER MORE.
!!

AND THEN YOU TELL HER THAT YOU HATE IT.
......

SAATI!
ガタ
ガタ
PLEASE, COME BACK!

DON'T WASTE YOUR BREATH. SHE'S NOT COMING BACK AFTER THAT.

FINALLY, IT'S JUST ME AND HITOSHI...
...NOW, HE'LL HAVE NO CHOICE BUT TO PAY ATTENTION TO ME.

NUMBER THIRTY?
ARE YOU THERE?
ERROR
Bleep

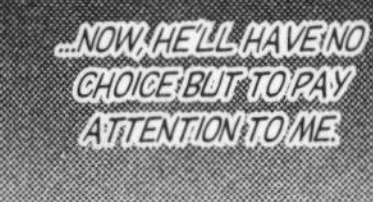

CRAP.
ERROR
Bleep
SAATI, CAN YOU HEAR ME?
PLEASE, LET ME SEE YOU.

Boop
ERROR !!
DAMN, I CAN'T EVEN TELL HER I'M SORRY.
I'M SORRY, SAATI. I'M SORRY.
CAN WE TALK? PLEASE?
PLEASE... I'M BEGGING YOU.
HMPH.
I'M NOT EVEN LISTENING.
WHAT ABOUT DINNER? WHAT DO I DO?
THAT REMINDS ME... WHAT'S HE GOING TO DO ABOUT DINNER?
OH, HITOSHI!

DINNER'S READY!
HUH?
どどーん
W-WHAT'S ALL THIS?
SNAPPING TURTLE STEW... AND PIT VIPER SOUP.
THERE'S ALSO GRILLED EEL AND A SURPRISE GARLIC DISH.
WHAAT?
I MADE IT FOR OUR SPECIAL EVENING TONIGHT.
HUH?!
EAT UP. YOU'LL NEED LOTS OF ENERGY.

...!!
HEY, WHAT'S THIS?
A BILL?!
DON'T TELL ME YOU HAD THIS STUFF DELIVERED!
Bill of service
Mr. Kobe
42300
料理代として
The customer listed is responsible for paying the amount in full.
IS THAT BAD?
WELL, DUH! THAT'S EVEN WORSE THAN HAVING TO EAT SOMETHING *YOU* MADE!
AND HOW CAN YOU THINK ABOUT FOOD AT A TIME LIKE THIS?!
WHOOPS.
...?!
WHY DO I FEEL SO RELIEVED?
Bleep
ERROR
I GUESS IT'S NO USE.
IT DOESN'T MATTER HOW BADLY I WANT TO APOLOGIZE TO HER.
......

SAATI, I KNOW THIS IS MY FAULT!
I WAS WRONG TO SAY ALL THOSE THINGS!
IT'S JUST... I DON'T KNOW HOW GIRLS THINK!
I WISH I COULD TAKE IT BACK!
......
PLEASE, JUST GIVE ME A CHANCE!
PLEASE?
HITOSHI-SAN...

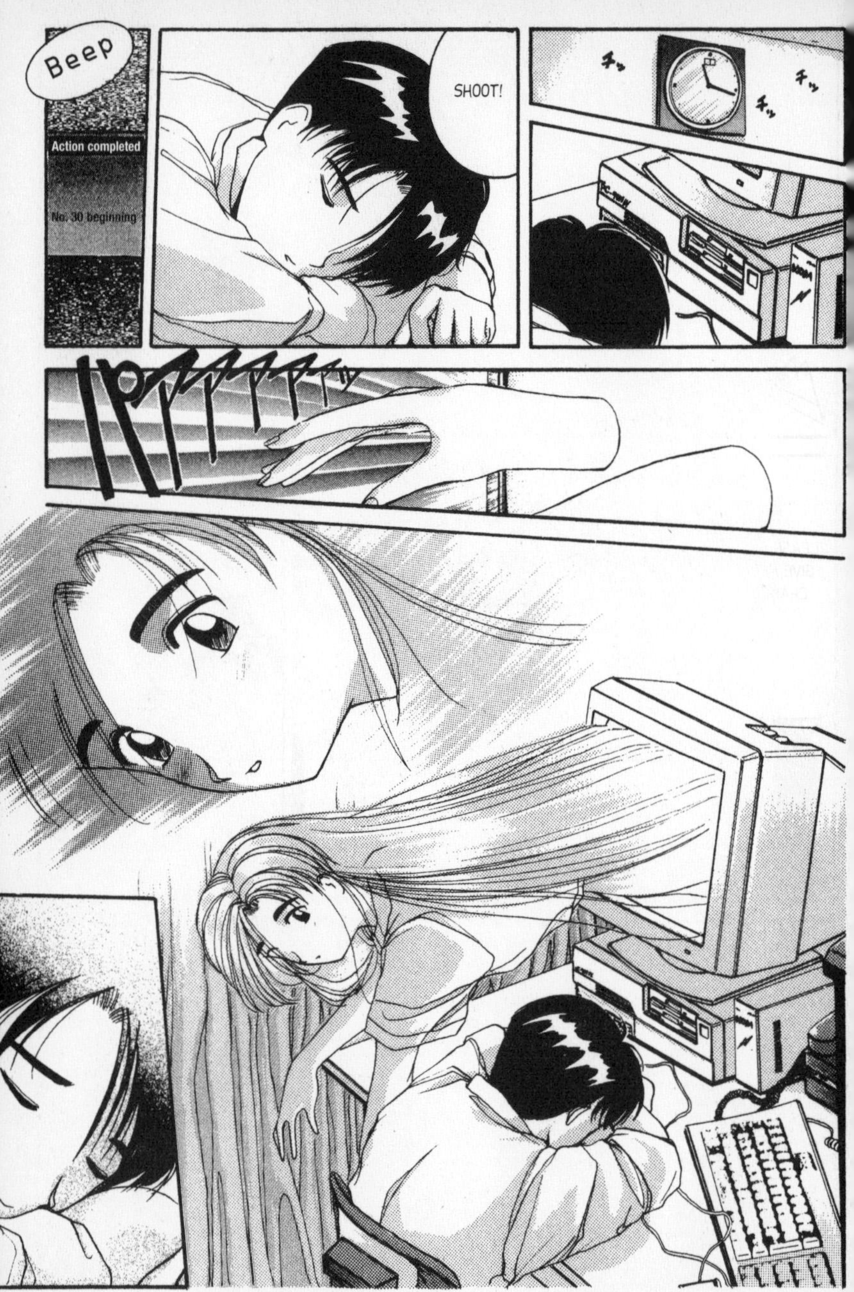
チッ
チッ
チッ
SHOOT!
Beep
Action completed
No. 30 beginning

ソーッ
フワッ
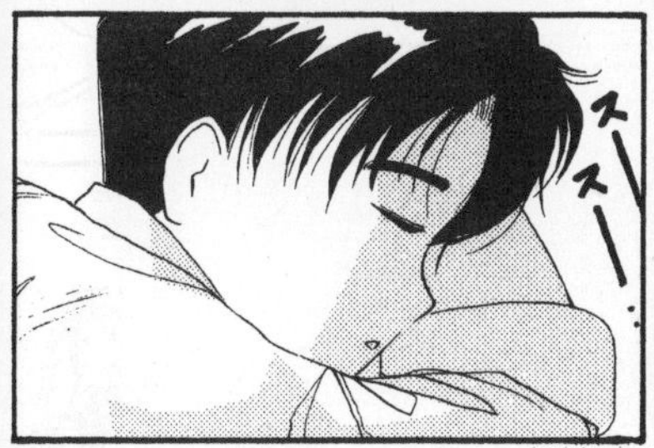
スー
スー

......

YOU'LL CATCH COLD WITHOUT A BLANKET.
HITOSHI-SAN, YOU SILLY BOY.

パサッ

スッ
くすっ
MMM...SORRY, SAATI... I...MMNN.
HITOSHI-SAN...
...I DON'T KNOW WHAT I WAS THINKING.
YOU CREATED ME. YOU TAUGHT ME SO MUCH.
AND EVEN THOUGH I SHOULD BE THANKFUL...
I GUESS...SHE'S BETTER FOR YOU THAN I AM.
...WHENEVER I SEE YOU AND SIS TOGETHER...
...I GET SO FRUS-TRATED AND SAD.
CHU♡
....
I DON'T HAVE WHAT IT TAKES TO BE YOUR GIRLFRIEND.

THAT'S RIGHT.
YOU FINALLY GET IT.
OH...
...SIS? YOU HEARD?!
UH, WHA--?!
SAATI, YOU'RE HERE?!
バッ
AHH!
I'M SORRY, I--
タッ
WAIT!!
グッ
DON'T LEAVE YET!!
JUST LET ME EXPLAIN SOMETHING FIRST!!

A LONG TIME AGO, I DID ASK TONI TO BE MY GIRLFRIEND.
STOP IT, HITOSHI-SAN! I DON'T WANNA HEAR ANYMORE!
SURE, I LIKE GIRLS WITH BIG BOOBS AND LONG LEGS! BUT WHAT GUY DOESN'T?!
AH HA HA HA!!
WELL, I CAN'T COMPLAIN ABOUT YOUR TASTE!
BUT I NEVER **INTENDED** TO ASK HER TO BE MY GIRLFRIEND...
WHAT?
...UNTIL TWENTY SAID...
I CAN ONLY FUNCTION IN EITHER "GIRLFRIEND" OR "BULLY" MODE.
WHICH DO YOU PREFER?
SHE GAVE ME NO CHOICE.
ALL RIGHT, BE MY GIRLFRIEND!
....
SAATI, YOU MIGHT NOT HAVE BEEN DESIGNED LIKE TONI WAS...
...BUT YOU'RE THE ONE I WANT BY MY SIDE.
I NEED YOU, SAATI.

IT'S STRANGE...
...HEARING HITOSHI'S WORDS...
...IT SOMEHOW MADE MY HEART FEEL BETTER.
HITOSHI-SAN, I FORGIVE YOU!
THANK YOU, SAATI. THANK YOU.
HEY...
...HOLD UP!!
WHAT ABOUT *ME*, HUH?! WHAT AM I?!
I'M SORRY, TONI.
JUST SHUT THE HELL UP!

APPARENTLY, YOU'RE STILL NOT AWARE OF MY SUPERIORITY.
ALLOW ME TO DEMONSTRATE ONCE AGAIN!!
TAKE *THAT!!*
ドカーン
KYAAAAAH!
もくもく
HITOSHI-SAN?!
HITOSHI-SAN?!
SORRY, GIRL, BUT I'M TAKING HITOSHI WITH ME.
IF YOU'VE GOT A PROBLEM WITH THAT, YOU'D BETTER DEAL. BYE NOW!
SIS, YOU CAN'T!!

THE WORLD OF A.I. LOVE YOU

LOVE TALK!

KEN AKAMATSU TELLS ALL

Musings from Ken Akamatsu about how unique characters are key to telling captivating stories!!

KEN AKAMATSU Special talk

Number Twenty makes her first appearance in the second volume. What do you think is special about her character?

Akamatsu: Twenty and Saati were made using different programming languages. Twenty was made with Assembly language, which makes her very streamlined and simple. Saati, on the other hand, has a "feedback function" that allows her to learn and change herself. Saati was made in the C programming language which allows her to be more flexible and adaptable than Twenty. Unfortunately, Twenty doesn't learn and progress like Saati, and this means that Saati will likely become more powerful than Twenty. Still, Twenty will always get higher marks when it comes to physical appearance.

Twenty and Saati were made...

In this volume, I think that the contrast in characters is very strong. The differences in programming languages actually helped the character's personalities to be even more different. It's like if Saati does this, then Twenty would have to do this.

Twenty is very similar to Aso-san's character, isn't she?

Akamatsu: Yes, she is. Hitoshi-san used Aso-san as a model for Number Twenty. Since he couldn't have Aso-san, he just decided to re-create her. He was also very fixated on breasts at the time.

Has A.I. Love You had any influence on your work with Love Hina?

Akamatsu: It sure has. There's a scene in A.I. Love You where Saati screams that Hitoshi is a pervert and starts hitting him. In Love Hina, there are quite a few similar scenes where Naru says and does the exact same thing to Keitaro.

...using different programming languages.

What about the cover of the second book?

Akamatsu: Since it's an ocean scene again, I wondered if the cover would work all right. I thought about setting it in outer space, but that seemed a little too hard. (laughs) The concept is that she's swimming inside the World Wide Web, so the image illustrates that idea. I hope you're looking forward to the third volume.

AH HA HA HA!! SORRY, SISTER, BUT IF YOU DON'T LIKE IT...
...WHY DON'T YOU TRY AND TAKE HIM BACK?!
HITOSHI-SAN!
NGGH!
AAHHH!
?
ゴホ
ゴホ
WAIT, WHAT'S THIS?!
MAP
The map on the right shows our location.
If you think you've got what it takes, then come and face me! You'll only lose anyway! Ha ha ha!!

A.I. LOVE YOU

Program.14 Saati VS Toni

OOFF!!
OWW OWW OWWIE!
FINALLY, ALONE AT LAST.
SO, HITOSHI. YOU READY?

WHA--?!
HEH HEH.
W-WHAT ARE YOU GONNA DO?!

OH, THERE'S NO USE RESISTING. YOU'RE NOT GOING ANYWHERE..

NO--DON'T LEAVE ME TIED UP!

I DON'T THINK YOU GET IT.

YOU...AND I...ARE GOING TO HAVE...
...A LITTLE LATE NIGHT FUN!
AN AMUSEMENT PARK?

Beep
THE LITTLE GIRL'S HERE.
AH!
YOU MEAN SAATI?!
WAIT, ISN'T THIS...
...THE PORT-SIDE AMUSEMENT PARK?
SO, SHE ACTUALLY CAME, DID SHE?! WELL, NO WORRY...
...THIS PLACE IS TOTALLY UNDER MY CONTROL!
CLOSE THE GATE!
I DON'T WANT ANY INTRUDERS!
NO, DON'T DO IT!!
HUH?
KYAAAH!

AW, TOO BAD. THE GATE'S LOCKED!
SAATI, THANK GOD!!
OOH, THE STAFF ENTRANCE IS OPEN.
NOT BAD, LITTLE SISTER!
NOT BAD AT ALL!!
SIS! HITOSHI-SAN!!
WHERE ARE YOU?!
WELCOME TO TONILAND, DEAR SISTER!
ARE YOU WOMAN ENOUGH TO FACE ME?!

I'M IN THE PENGUIN CASTLE!
IF YOU WANT HITOSHI, THEN COME AND *GET* HIM!
NO, SAATI! DON'T DO IT!!
HUH?
IT'S A TRAP!
HITOSHI-SAN'S THERE?!
JUST HANG ON! I'M COMING!!
ダッ
PENGUIN CASTLE, DEAD AHEAD!
Penguin Castle
This way 100 meters
STUPID GIRL, SHE WALKED RIGHT INTO MY TRAP. NOW TO TURN UP THE HEAT.
GET READY FOR A **MELTDOWN!**
AH!
YEESS!!
I CALL THIS ...
...THE BAHAMUT HELLFIRE STRATEGY!!
NO!!
YOU CAN'T!

ゴウン…
ゴーゴー
ムアア アアア
YES, VERY SOON THE HEART OF THIS CASTLE WILL BECOME A BLAZING FURNACE!!
THAT AIR-HEADED DITZ WILL BE STEAMED ALIVE!! BWA HA HA HA!!
うろうろ
HEH HEH.
キョロキョロ
THAT'S STRANGE.
WHY ISN'T SHE SUFFER-ING?
!!
IT'S A BIT CHILLY IN HERE.
Haunted House
ARGH!!
THAT CLUE-LESS DITZ WENT THE WRONG FREAKIN' WAY!

AHH!

WHOA! TONI, WHAT'S WRONG?!

Heating System

ARE YOU HURT?

UGH, I ALMOST HAD THE MELT-DOWN.

HOT

I FORGOT TO TAKE INTO ACCOUNT THAT HEAT RISES.

UM, CAN WE GO HOME NOW?

AH...HER GOING INTO THE HAUNTED HOUSE WAS A STROKE OF LUCK.

ALL OF THE GHOSTS ARE UNDER MY CONTROL!

I'LL SCARE THE TWERP TO DEATH AND THEN STRING HER UP IN THERE! BWA HA HA HA!!

WHERE AM I? THIS DOESN'T SEEM LIKE PENGUIN CASTLE.
Here Lies M. May
Ancestral grave
HITOSHI-SAN! SIS!
WWAAARRRGHHH!!

LOOK, SHE'S SCARED. SHE'S ACTUALLY SCARED! HA HA HA!

OH NO, SIS!
WHAT HAP-PENED?! YOU LOOK TERRIBLE!

OH? WAIT A MINUTE, THIS ISN'T SIS...

...BUT IT *IS* ONE OF OUR KIND.

PLEASE, EVERY-ONE...
...TELL ME WHERE HITOSHI-SAN IS.
......
THEY'RE THAT WAY?!
THANK YOU SO MUCH!
ドッ
AHHHH! MR. GHOST!!
YOU DIRTY TRAITOR!
HOW *DARE* YOU SIDE WITH THE ENEMY?!
ズラッ
WHY ARE YOU DOING THIS, SIS?!

ENOUGH JABBERING! YOU'VE GOT AN ELITE ARMY OF ROBOT PIRATES TO DEAL WITH!
GO AHEAD. TAKE 'ER DOWN, BOYS!!
GAAH!!
DAMMIT! YOU STUPID PIECES OF CRAP!
GOTTA GET LONGER CORDS NEXT TIME!!
SHUT YOUR TRAP! NOW, SILVER, COME!!
HIYAAHH!!
SIS, WHY DO YOU KEEP DOING ALL OF THIS?!

HA HA HA!
AH, BUT--
IF YOU THINK YOU CAN CATCH US, THEN GO AHEAD AND *TRY!*
SAATI!
...
WHA--?!
I'LL ADMIT, THAT WAS PRETTY FAST.
NOW WHO'S THE AIRHEAD?!
SIS, PLEASE--LET HITOSHI-SAN GO!
AIN'T GONNA HAPPEN!
I'M A SUPERIOR MODEL. WHY SHOULD I HAVE TO GIVE IN TO YOU?
ALL I'M LOOKING TO DO IS HAVE A GOOD TIME WITH HITOSHI! SO DON'T GET IN MY WAY, GIRL!

TONIGHT WE'RE GONNA RIDE ON THIS, HITOSHI!
TH-THAT?!
WHY, YES! IT'S THE MOST POPULAR RIDE IN THE PARK.
THE *SCREAM MACHINE* ROLLER COASTER.
UM, I HAVE THIS THING...
...ABOUT ROLLER COASTERS. HOW ABOUT ANOTHER RIDE?
C'MON, THE FRONT'S SUPPOSED TO BE THE SCARIEST!
YOU'RE NOT EVEN LISTENING TO ME!
SAATI, STOP SPACING OUT AND COME SAVE ME!
ガタッ
OH MAN, IT MOVED!
I'M COMING, HITOSHI-SAN!
バッ

WARGH!
YOU STUBBORN LITTLE BRAT. CAN'T YOU LEAVE US ALONE FOR TEN WHOLE MINUTES?!
OH GOD, HERE IT COMES!!
BUT SIS--
GYAHH!!
HITOSHI AND I ARE LOVERS, SO JUST LEAVE!
YYAAHH!!
THAT'S ONLY BECAUSE YOU TRICKED HITOSHI INTO...
BWAARGHH!
AAARRGGHH!
WAAAGH!
...SAYING HE WANTED...
...YOU TO BE HIS--
WILL YOU SHUT UP?!
HITOSHI-SAN, I'M TRYING TO TALK HERE!
WHA--?!
WHY'D IT JUST STOP?!
OH GOD! I'M GONNA DIE!!
HITOSHI-SAN?!

KYAH!
AH!
KYAH!
EEEK!
がしっ
JEEZ, C'MON NOW!!
SOMEBODY'S GONNA HAFTA LET GO!.
MMF!
ぶらーーん
WAAA!
HITOSHI-SAN! QUICK, CLIMB UP OVER US!
HUH?
UH, O-OKAY.
DON'T YOU EVEN TRY ANYTHING FUNNY!
UH, TOO LATE.
I CAN'T SAY THAT I'M ENJOYING THIS.

I JUST SAW MY LIFE FLASH BEFORE MY EYES.
QUIT YAPPING AND HELP US UP ALREADY!!
OKAY, UPS-A-DAISY!
UH OH!
AAHHHH!
?!
HITOSHI-SAN?!
YOU... SAVED US?!

UH...
...SO... HEAVY.
YOU CAN DO IT, HITOSHI-SAN!
DON'T LEGGO! DON'T LEGGO!
OH MAN...
...THE HINGES.
P-PLEASE...
...HURRY AND PULL US UP!
I'M...TRYING, BUT...
...MY ARM'S GONE...NUMB.
IT'S NO USE...
THEY'RE BOTH GONNA FALL IF I DON'T DO SOMETHING.
I'LL HAVE TO LET GO OF ONE OF THEM...
...NO, HOW DO I EVEN MAKE THAT DECISION?!

HITOSHI-SAN...
...THERE ISN'T MUCH TIME.
ッチラッ
UHH...
...IF I DIE I'M COMIN' BACK TO HAUNT YOU!
ザク
ザク
ザク
ALL I'M LOOKING TO DO IS HAVE A GOOD TIME WITH HITOSHI!
......
I CAN'T...
...HOLD ON ANY LONGER.
?!
HITOSHI-SAN...
...TAKE CARE OF...
...MY SISTER FOR ME.
ぱっ

?!
SAATI!!
ザシィッ
!

KYAAAAH!
DON'T JUST HANG THERE...
...HURRY UP AND CLIMB UP!
SI-SIS?!
TONI...CAUGHT SAATI?
OWWIE OUUCH OWW!!
YOU SAVED ME, SIS.
THANK YOU SO MUCH!
HMPH.
I'M NOT GONNA LET YOU PLAY THE "GOOD GIRL" BY SACRIFICING YOURSELF.

BESIDES I DON'T BUY IT.
WHY WOULD YOU GIVE UP YOUR LIFE TO SAVE THIS CRYBABY?
ハッ
YOU BEAT ME FAIR AND SQUARE.
SO I DON'T CARE. YOU CAN HAVE HITOSHI.
I'M NOT INTO AIRHEADS...
...BUT YOU'RE MADE FOR EACH OTHER.
WELL SEE YA.
I'LL BE OUT OF YOUR HAIR NOW.
THANKS, SIS.
YEAH, TONI'S A GOOD ONE.
Yet, just when they thought the storm had passed...
WHAT ARE YOU DOING IN MY HOUSE?!
WELL, I DON'T HAVE ANYWHERE ELSE TO GO.

A.I. Love You – Cover Production

We take a look at the how a cover is made!

First Process

This is the process Ken Akamatsu uses to take an image from his mind and bring it to life on a blank sheet of paper.

A. First, I draw a rough sketch illustrating the concept of the characters floating in the web. Then, the main lines are filled in with pencil.

B. Pencil shading gives the drawing a warmer feel. And when dealing with a color illustration, I never use pen.

Second Process

I scan the pencil drawing and transfer it to a P.C., where I then start the colorization process. This is the step that really shows how useful a computer can be.

C. I use a program called Painter to add color. It gives the illusion that you actually used a brush.

D. I don't use Adobe Photoshop because it actually tends to create a rough texture. And I especially try to avoid using the brush tool.

Text By Ken Akamatsu

A.I.
LOVE YOU
Program.15
Mountain Happening

ALL RIGHT, HERE WE GO!
ギュッ
QUICK, HITOSHI! LOOK!!
HUH?
TA-DAH!
UWAHH!
WELL, SUMMER VACA-TION HAS STARTED, RIGHT?
LET'S GO TO THE BEACH!
THE GLOWING RAYS, THE SPARKLING OCEAN AND THE HOT GUYS!

HEH HEH! NICE, ISN'T IT?
YEAH, THAT'S FINE BUT WHAT'S WITH THE BIKINI?
OH, SIS! WHAT A CUTE BATHING SUIT.
ISN'T IT, THOUGH?
SUMMER VACATION IS HERE. LET'S GO TO THE BEACH!
IT WAS ON SALE, SO I JUST... BOUGHT IT.
JEEZ, IT'S HIDEOUS.
BUT, SIS, MY SENSEI TOLD ME...
...I SHOULDN'T WASTE MY SUMMER BREAK FOOLING AROUND.
SO, I WENT AHEAD AND MADE "HITOSHI-SAN'S DAILY SCHEDULE"! YAY!
HITOSHI-SAN
Bathing
Studying
Studying
Shopping
Potty
Cleaning
Computer Programming
HEY, HOLD UP! YOU DIDN'T LEAVE HIM ANY FREE TIME!!
AND WHAT ABOUT EATING AND SLEEPING?
OOPS, IT'S ALREADY TWO! TIME TO STUDY.
OKAY, HITOSHI-SAN. LET'S GO.
UHH ...
NO WAY! LET'S GO TO THE BEACH!!

WELL, ACTUALLY, I WAS THINKING...
...ABOUT GOING TO THE MOUNTAINS TOMORROW.
THE MOUNTAINS?
DID YOU SAY STARS ARE GOING TO FALL ON US?!
WE CAN'T BE HERE! WE'LL BE CRUSHED!!
NO, NOT ON EARTH. ON JUPITER.
YOU SEE, ALL THIS WEEK...
...PIECES OF A COMET ARE GOING TO CRASH INTO JUPITER.
WHEN THEY DO, JUPITER'S GRAVITATIONAL FORCE IS GOING TO BREAK THEM INTO DOZENS OF SMALLER PIECES.
AND THEN ONE AFTER ANOTHER THEY'LL ALL COME CRASHING DOWN.

*Comet Shoemaker - Levy 9, named for its discoverers.

THIS ONLY HAPPENS, LIKE, ONCE EVERY THOUSAND YEARS.
THAT'S WHY WE'RE HERE.
BUT WHAT'S THE POINT OF OBSERVING THE STARS?
YOU AND I ARE IN THE ASTRONOMY CLUB, REMEMBER?!
THIS MOUNTAIN IS PERFECT FOR STARGAZING.
THAT MAKES SENSE.
ザワ
ザワ
ザワ
MAN, THERE ARE A LOT OF PEOPLE.
MAYBE THEY'RE ALL HERE FOR THE SAME REASON.
HUH?
HEY, THEY'RE HAVING A PHOTO CONTEST.
tronomy Photo
Contest
Prizes
DANG, ALL THE GOOD SPOTS ARE ALREADY TAKEN.
YOOHOO, HITOSHI!!
THERE'S A GOOD SPOT OPEN OVER HERE!
YEAH, THAT WORKS.

WE REALLY LUCKED OUT UP HERE.
COME ON. LET'S GET SET UP.
AH HA HA HA!!
HUH? THAT VOICE...?
FANCY MEET-ING YOU HERE, KOBE-KUN.
YOU EXPECTING TO DO SOME STARGAZING?
KIMIKA-SAN?!
IS THAT YOU?!
WHO'S THE CHICK?
KIMIKA-SAN. SHE'S ONE OF OUR CLASS-MATES.
WHAT ARE YOU DOING HERE?
WHAT DO YOU MEAN BY THAT? THIS IS MY SUMMER HOME.

AND YOU HAPPEN TO BE STANDING IN MY GARDEN.
I...I DIDN'T KNOW!!
I ALWAYS SPEND MY SUMMER HIDING OUT HERE.
BUT THIS YEAR, THERE'S ALL THIS FUSS ABOUT SOME METEORS OR SOMETHING.
I'M NOT REALLY INTO THIS STUFF, BUT I FIGURED, WHAT THE HECK.
?!
OH MY GOD! THAT TELESCOPE HAS A BUILT-IN SKY SENSOR AND INTERLOCKING REFLECTIVE LENSES!
I'D KILL FOR THAT BABY!
HEY, KIMIKA-SAN? CAN I SEE THAT FOR A SEC?
WHAT?
PLEASE! I'VE NEVER SEEN THIS KIND BEFORE.
ONLY A PRINCESS COULD AFFORD THIS BEAUTY.
WELL, I GUESS SO. YOU DID JUST CALL ME A PRINCESS, AFTER ALL.
REALLY?! YOU MEAN IT?!

HEY, HITOSHI...
...QUIT TALKING TO THAT BITCH AND GET OVER HERE.
WAIT A SEC!
YOU'RE THAT GIRL FROM THE OTHER DAY!
LOOK, LADY--
I NEVER FORGET A FACE!!
YOU GUYS KNOW EACH OTHER?
NO, WE DON'T!
GRRRRRRR!!
THIS BITCH STOLE THE SWIMSUIT THAT I'D PICKED OUT THE OTHER DAY!
IT PISSES ME OFF JUST THINKING ABOUT IT!
WHAT THE HELL ARE YOU TALKING ABOUT?! I HAD IT FIRST!
SUMMER SPECIAL!! SWIMSUIT SALE
キャ!
KOBE-KUN, IS SHE A FRIEND OF YOURS OR SOMETHING?!
UM, ACTUALLY... SHE'S SAATI'S OLDER SISTER.

OH, THAT EXPLAINS IT! I THOUGHT SHE WAS A SKANK
THE LITTLE SKANK IS JUST FOLLOWING HER SISTER'S LEAD...
...IN TRYING TO MAKE A FOOL OUT OF ME!
HARD TO BELIEVE THE LITTLE PRINCESS IS SO CHEAP...
...SHE'D FIGHT OVER A BIKINI!
WHAT?!
WHAT'D YOU SAY?
THAT BIKINI WAS PERFECT FOR ME!
PRINCESS, NOTHING WOULD EVER LOOK GOOD ON YOU.
UM, GUYS?
WHY DON'T WE JUST PLAY WITH THE TELESCOPE?
YOU THINK I'LL STILL SHARE IT NOW?!
パチバチッ
YOU'RE BANNED FOR LIFE!!
TONI, YOU NEED TO WORK ON THOSE PEOPLE SKILLS.
WE COULD'VE BEEN SET FOR THIS WHOLE WEEKEND ...

...INSTEAD OF BEING STUCK WITH THIS TELESCOPE.
JEEZ, HOW AM I GOING TO GET ANY GOOD PICTURES NOW?
MAYBE WE SHOULD JUST FORGET ABOUT IT AND GO BACK HOME.
DON'T SAY THAT, HITOSHI-SAN!
THE SIZE OF YOUR TELESCOPE ISN'T EVERYTHING, IS IT?
IF WE HANG IN THERE, I BET WE CAN GET SOME NICE SHOTS.
BESIDES, I WANT YOU TO TEACH ME ABOUT STARGAZING.
HUNH.
I GUESS YOU'RE RIGHT.
WE DID COME ALL THIS WAY.
IT'S NICE TO HAVE SAATI ALWAYS STANDING BY ME.
IT'S A GOOD FEELING.
OKAY, THE TELESCOPE'S ALL SET UP.
NOW, LETS SET UP CAMP.
YOU GOT IT!

UHHH...
...WHAT'S ALL THIS CRAP?!
バババァン
WHY DO WE HAVE A TV AND INFLATABLE WHALE HERE?!
W-WHAT HAPPENED TO THE TENT AND...FOOD?
Windy
OH, YOU DIDN'T HAVE ANYTHING FUN PACKED. SO I JUST SWITCHED IT ALL.
WHY THE HELL DID YOU EVEN COME?!
EHH?
A FISHING POLE?
NOW WE'VE GOT NO CHOICE BUT TO GO HOME.
AH, IT FIGURES.
EH HEH HEH.
HOW LONG DOES THIS TAKE?
I HOPE WE CAN CATCH SOME DINNER.
キリ キリ キリ

IT FEELS KINDA REFRESHING TO BE OUT HERE, HUH?
YES, AND THIS IS A NICE SPOT.
YEAH, IT IS.
ピクッ
AH, HITOSHI-SAN. LOOK!
YOU'VE GOT ONE!!
I DO?!
ALL RIGHT!!
HERE COMES DINNER!
OWW, DAMMIT! STOP!!

YOU JERK! WHAT ARE YOU TRYIN' TO DO?
AND IT WAS SUCH A NICE SWIM TOO
WHOSE FAULT IS IT THAT WE DON'T HAVE ANY FOOD?!
JEEZ, I GET IT ALREADY.
I'LL GO OUT AND LOOK FOR FOOD ALSO.
ALL RIGHT!
WE'VE GOT DINNER!
IT'S GET-TING LATE. WHERE DID TONI GO?
OH, ARE YOU WORRIED ABOUT ME?
LOOK.
HOW WILL THESE DO?
WHOA!!
TOMATOES, CORN... EVEN SOME WATERMELON!
WOW, YOU REALLY FOUND ALL THIS?
OF COURSE. WHAT'D YOU EXPECT?
'KAY, LET'S DIG...
...HUH?
HAM?
CANS? UM...
WHY ARE THERE CANS?

...ACTUALLY, THERE'S A HOUSE OVER THERE.
NOBODY WAS THERE, SO I JUST RAIDED THEIR FRIDGE. THAT COOL?
NO, IT'S NOT COOL! THAT'S SOME-ONE'S CABIN!! AND IT'S CALLED STEALING!
WE CAN'T DO ANYTHING ABOUT WHAT WE ATE...
...BUT AT LEAST, WE CAN TAKE BACK THE REST.
WHY IS TONI RUIN-ING EVERY-THING?!
MAN, WHAT A HUGE THICKET.
OH, WHAT'S THIS?
HUH?
WHAT'S WHAT?
WHOA!
THAT'S A HOT SPRING!
WHAT'S A HOT SPRING?
IT'S LIKE A NATURAL BATH. IT'S HOT, BUT GOOD.

WOW, TO THINK NOBODY HAS CLAIMED THIS THING YET.
I BET ALL THE ANIMALS AROUND HERE LOVE USING IT.
HUH?
WHA--?!
ぬぎっ
ALL RIGHT!
WHHHAAA?! WHAT'RE YOU DOING?!
WHAT ARE YOU SCREAMIN' ABOUT NOW?!
WE CAN'T JUST IGNORE THIS LITTLE GEM.
C'MON, LET'S GO GET WARMED UP.
UM, BUT, UH, THAT MIGHT...
...UH, HEY, SAATI?
AHH, THIS IS NICE.
WHAT THE?! SAAATTIIII?!
C'MON, HITOSHI. DON'T BE SHY!
ドボーン
UWAAAAARGHH!!

AHHHH.
YOU WERE RIGHT, HITOSHI-SAN. THIS SURE FEELS GOOD.
YEAH, THAT IT DOES.
MMM, I'M IN HEAVEN.
NOTHIN' BEATS A SUMMER IN THE MOUNTAINS.
AND SHE BEGGED TO GO TO THE BEACH.
OOH, LOOK!
THE STARS ARE OUT.
DID YOU KNOW THAT BRIGHT STAR OVER THERE ISN'T JUPITER?
IT'S ACTUALLY VENUS. AND AT THIS HOUR, IT'S ALWAYS THE BRIGHTEST AND THE PRETTIEST.

BUT GET THIS-- THAT'S ACTU-ALLY VENUS FROM THREE MINUTES AGO.
WHAT DO YOU MEAN?

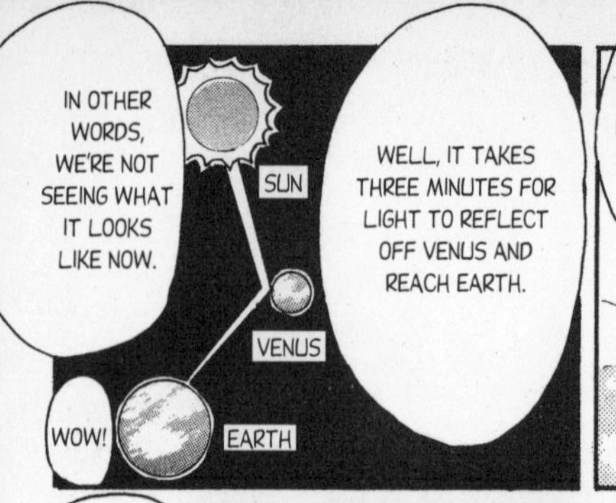
WELL, IT TAKES THREE MINUTES FOR LIGHT TO REFLECT OFF VENUS AND REACH EARTH.
SUN
VENUS
EARTH
IN OTHER WORDS, WE'RE NOT SEEING WHAT IT LOOKS LIKE NOW.
WOW!

YEP, AND THE LIGHT FROM SIRIUS IS ACTUALLY FROM 8.7 YEARS AGO.

THINK ABOUT IT. SPACE IS OVER 20 BILLION YEARS OLD...
...AND I'VE ONLY BEEN HERE FOR 16 YEARS.

WHEN I THINK OF IT THAT WAY...
...IT JUST MAKES ALL THE LITTLE THINGS SEEM INCON-SEQUENTIAL.

MAYBE THAT'S WHY I LIKE LOOKING AT THE STARS SO MUCH.

AHHHH.

IT'S SO PRETTY.

I THINK I UNDER-STAND WHY PEOPLE...
...LIKE STAR-GAZING SO MUCH.
チャプーン
HMM?
スゥッ
?!
SOME-THING'S IN HERE!
Beware of Bears
WAIT, DIDN'T I READ THAT BEARS ARE STILL IN THE AREA?
WHAT IS IT?
SHHH!
QUIET! IT MIGHT BE A BEAR!

SLOWLY NOW.
LEAVIN'...
...AWREADY?!
ARGH!
IT'S A BEAR!!
JEEZ, ASO-SAN! YOU SCARED US...
...HALF TO DEATH!
WHO ARE YOU CALLING A BEAR?
HUH?
DID YOU COME HERE TO BATHE TOO?
WHAT?
WHEN WILL YOU PEOPLE EVER LEARN?!
THIS IS MY FAMILY'S HOT SPRING!
YOU'RE KIDDING!
WAIT, THAT'S OUR STOLEN FOOD!!
SO, YOU WERE THE ONES WHO TOOK IT!!

THE NERVE OF YOU PEOPLE!! FIRST YOU STEAL FROM ME...
...THEN YOU USE MY BATH WITHOUT PERMISSION!!
NOW YOU LOOK HERE.
THERE'S NO SIGN ON THIS HOT SPRING. AND THAT FOOD WAS JUST SITTING THERE. SO, WE ATE IT.
WHAT KIND OF AN EXCUSE IS THAT?!
WHO THE HELL DO YOU THINK YOU ARE?
YOU'D BETTER APOLOGIZE!
FOR A GIRL WITH SUCH A FANCY TELE-SCOPE YOU REALLY ARE A CHEAPSKATE.
WHAT WAS THAT?
S THAT SO?
OKAY THEN, HOW ABOUT A LITTLE WAGER?
HITOSHI'S TELESCOPE MIGHT BE A PIECE OF CRAP...
...BUT I BET HE CAN TAKE BET-TER PICTURES THAN YOU.

WE'LL ENTER OUR PHOTOS INTO THE CONTEST.
Astronomy Photo Contest
Prizes
To
IF KOBE-KUN WINS, I'LL FOR-GET ABOUT YOU STEALING MY STUFF.
HOWEVER...
...SHOULD I WIN...
...HITOSHI'S ASTRONOMY CLUB IS FINISHED!
HMM, SOUNDS INTERESTING.
WHA?!
YOU'RE ON!
UM, SAATI?
CAN YOU SAY SOME-THING?
HITOSHI-SAN LOVES ASTRONOMY! THERE'S NO WAY HE COULD EVER LOSE!!
YOU'VE GOT A DEAL!!
HUH?
WHAT?

A.I. Love You – Cover Production

We take a look at the how a cover is made!

Third Process

At this point, Mr. Akamatsu hands artwork over to the design department. They experiment with a few different backgrounds until they find the right one. And amazingly, there's only one more step before everything is complete.

E. It is the designer's job to come up with the perfect background and then overlay the characters on top of it. Needless to say, computers are very useful in this process.

F. The coloring and the outlines of the characters can then be adjusted if needed. This can also be done later on.

Final Process

During the final step, the ideal positions for the title logo and volume number are decided upon. The edges are then colored to fit the feeling and concept of the image. Luckily for the designer, this is where they get the chance to shine.

G. With a computer, the position of the logo can be altered ever so slightly until the right position is discovered.

H. If it is decided that the background doesn't quite work with the image, it can be quickly changed using a computer.

Text By Ken Akamatsu

A.I.
LOVE YOU
Program.16
A Wish Upon a Star

GOOD, IT'S SETTLED THEN. TONIGHT, JUPITER IS GOING TO GO THROUGH HELL...
...AND WE'LL BE RIGHT HERE WATCHING IT!
YOU HEARD THE RULES. YOU WIN THE ASTRONOMY CONTEST...
WHO THE HELL DO YOU THINK YOU ARE?
...AND I'LL FORGET EVERYTHING THAT'S HAPPENED.
BUT SHOULD I WIN...
...THE ASTRONOMY CLUB...
...WILL BE GONE *PERMANENTLY!!*
BUT--WHY CLOSE IT?!
YOU ONLY HAVE TWO MEMBERS. YOU DON'T EVEN ACCOMPLISH ANYTHING!
DON'T ACT LIKE YOU DON'T KNOW THE STUDENT BODY'S TRYING TO SHUT YOU DOWN.
Shut it down!
Stop now!
Shut it down!
Close it!
Shut down the astronomy club!
UGH.
I FORGOT. KIMIKA-SAN'S OUR STUDENT BODY REP.
I SUPPOSE YOU THOUGHT YOU'D ACCOMPLISH SOMETHING HERE...
...BUT I WONDER HOW WELL YOU'LL DO.

IF YOU LOSE TO A TOTAL NOVICE LIKE ME...
...IT'S ONLY NATURAL THAT YOU'D WANT TO SHUT IT DOWN.

....
16t

Astronomy Photo Contest
EH HEH HEH!

THIS SURE TURNED INTO A BIG ORDEAL.
IT DID?
BUT WE CAN DO IT!

OUR EQUIPMENT MIGHT NOT BE UP TO PAR...
...BUT THERE'S NO WAY I'M GOING TO SHUT DOWN OUR CLUB!

KIMIKA-SAN SAID IT HERSELF...
...SHE'S A NOVICE, AND I'LL PROVE IT!

ALL RIGHT! I'LL SHOW YOU THE POWER OF THE ASTRONOMY CLUB PRESIDENT.
WHOA!
HITOSHI-SAN'S ON FIRE!
ゴオオオオオオ
'KAY, LET'S GET CRACKIN'!
TIME TO UNLOAD THAT EQUIP-MENT!
ROGER THAT, HOUSTON!
HERE YOU GO.
UH, IS THAT ALL WE BROUGHT?
YEP, THE REST IS AT HOME.
WE LEFT THE SKY SENSOR AND THE INFRARED CAMERA AT HOME?!
'FRAID SO.
HEY, I BROUGHT MY CAMERA.
SEE?
IT'S A DISPOSABLE. NICE, HUH?

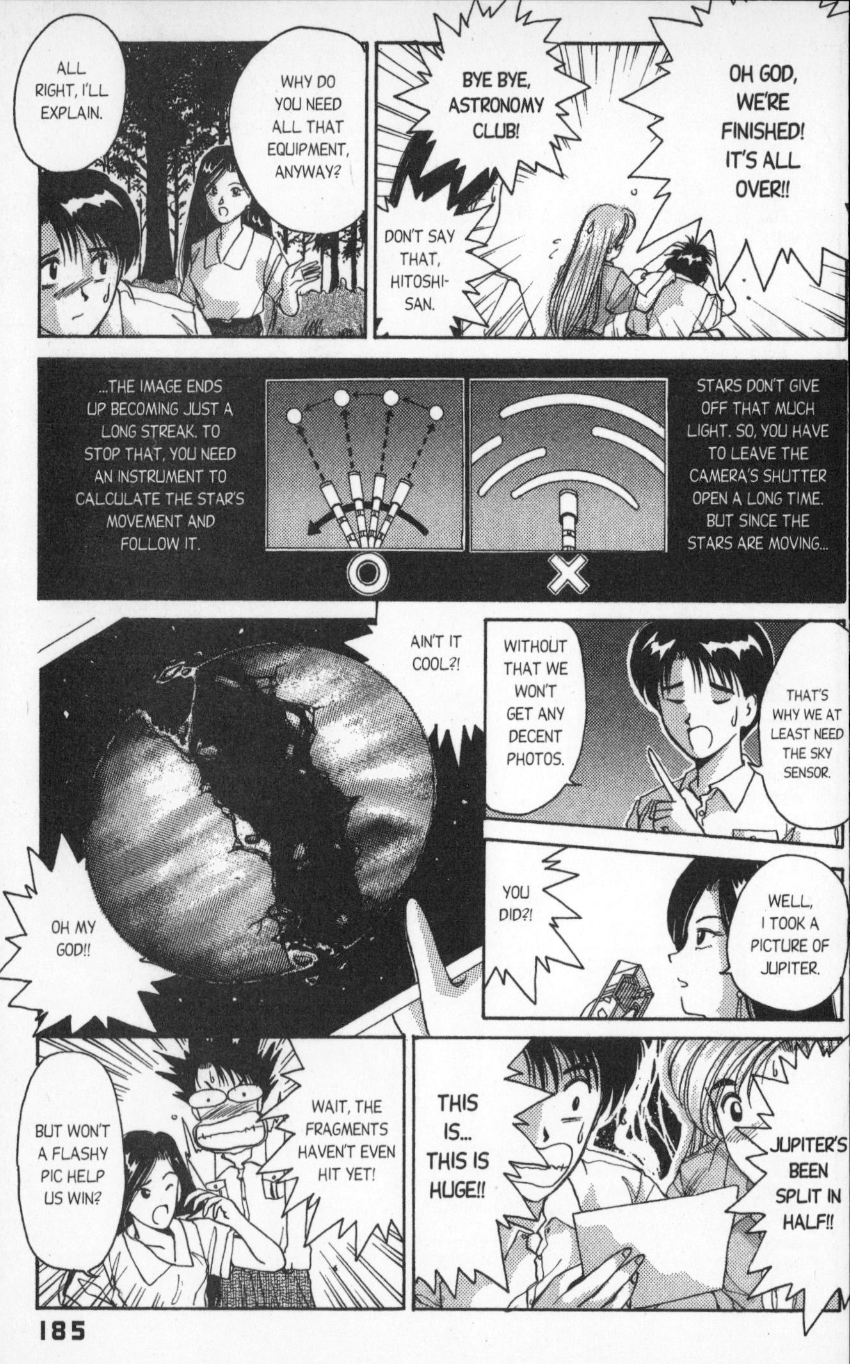
OH GOD, WE'RE FINISHED! IT'S ALL OVER!!
BYE BYE, ASTRONOMY CLUB!
DON'T SAY THAT, HITOSHI-SAN.
WHY DO YOU NEED ALL THAT EQUIPMENT, ANYWAY?
ALL RIGHT, I'LL EXPLAIN.
STARS DON'T GIVE OFF THAT MUCH LIGHT. SO, YOU HAVE TO LEAVE THE CAMERA'S SHUTTER OPEN A LONG TIME. BUT SINCE THE STARS ARE MOVING...
...THE IMAGE ENDS UP BECOMING JUST A LONG STREAK. TO STOP THAT, YOU NEED AN INSTRUMENT TO CALCULATE THE STAR'S MOVEMENT AND FOLLOW IT.
THAT'S WHY WE AT LEAST NEED THE SKY SENSOR.
WITHOUT THAT WE WON'T GET ANY DECENT PHOTOS.
WELL, I TOOK A PICTURE OF JUPITER.
YOU DID?!
AIN'T IT COOL?!
OH MY GOD!!
JUPITER'S BEEN SPLIT IN HALF!!
THIS IS... THIS IS HUGE!!
WAIT, THE FRAGMENTS HAVEN'T EVEN HIT YET!
BUT WON'T A FLASHY PIC HELP US WIN?

OH!
WELL, WELL, WELL. NICE SET-UP YOU'VE GOT THERE.
YOU REALLY THINK YOU CAN BEAT ME WITH *THAT* JUNK?
YOU MIGHT AS WELL JUST GIVE UP.
WE WON'T KNOW 'TIL WE TRY.
AH HA HA! IS THAT SO?
OH, MAN!
CHECK OUT THAT CAR!
YOU LIKE IT? IT'S MY DADDY'S CUSTOM-BUILT MOBILE OBSERVATORY.
I HAD IT SHIPPED UP HERE JUST FOR THIS LITTLE EVENT.
SO, YOU GUYS GET IT NOW?
YOU DON'T HAVE A CHANCE AGAINST ME!
DAMN.

AH, SCREW IT!
WE MIGHT AS WELL JUST QUIT!!

WE CAN'T WIN AGAINST A COMPUTERIZED TELESCOPE...
...WE DON'T EVEN HAVE ALL OUR EQUIPMENT!
IT'S IMPOS-SIBLE TO GET ANYTHING DECENT.
THIS SUCKS.

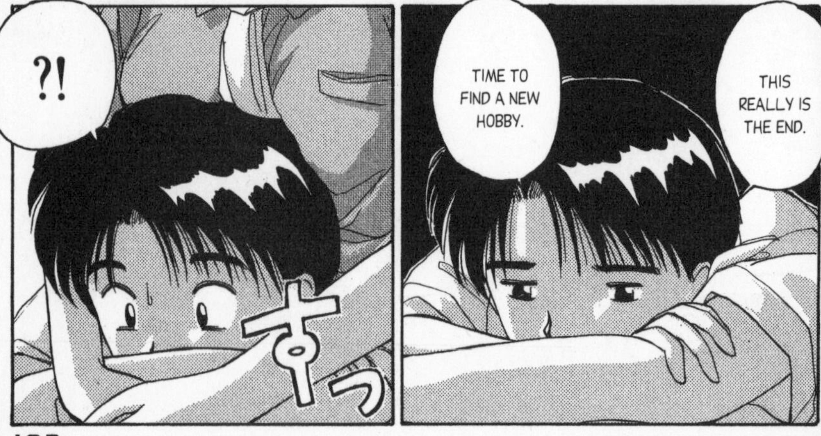
THIS REALLY IS THE END.
TIME TO FIND A NEW HOBBY.
?!
すっ

IF YOU KEEP YOUR HEAD DOWN...

...YOU'LL NEVER BE ABLE TO SEE THE STARS.

HUH?

Gluump!

DIDN'T YOU SAY THAT THE LITTLE THINGS WERE INCONSE-QUENTIAL?

YOU REMEM-BER THAT?

WOW!

YOU KNOW...

...SHE MIGHT HAVE A COMPUTERIZED MOBILE OBSERVATORY, BUT...

...YOU'VE GOT US. JUST THINK ABOUT IT.

FOR US, CALCULATING JUPITER'S ORBIT IS A PIECE OF CAKE.

JUST HANG IN THERE, HITOSHI-SAN!
WE'LL GET YOU THAT GREAT PICTURE!
YOU'RE RIGHT, SAATI.

THE PROBLEM ISN'T MY TELESCOPE.
IT'S MY ATTITUDE.
YEAH!
WE CAN DO THIS!
SAATI, FIND SOMETHING TO MOUNT THE CAMERA ONTO THE TELESCOPE!
YOU GOT IT!

Astronomy Photo Contest participants, please take your marks!

Soon, fragment D of Shoemaker-Levy 9 will be crashing into Jupiter!

And the question on everyone's mind is...

...who will capture the best moment of impact?

Ladies and gentlemen, let's all show our support!
Yes, this is a once in a lifetime opportunity...
カチッ
...and it's one that no one wants to
ワイ
So, good luck, everybody!!

YEP... THAT'S JUPITER ALL RIGHT.
OUR ONLY PROBLEM IS WHETHER OR NOT...
...WE CAN KEEP ITS PATH IN VIEW.

I RIGGED US A CABLE RELEASE BUTTON.
チャッ
NEXT, I JUST NEED TO CALCULATE THE EXACT TIME OF IMPACT.
CAN YOU GET ME JUPITER'S ORBIT AND MAKE THE TELESCOPE FOLLOW IT?
I CAN DO THAT.
JUST A SEC.

OH, AND...
...LET US GET A GOOD SHOT TOO.
PROGRAM OPTION NUMBER EIGHT!
CELESTIAL KNOWLEDGE, PLEASE STAY TRUE! KEEP JUPITER'S ORBIT IN VIEW!!
ヴー…ン

Bebleep
AND THAT'S THE FINAL COORDINATE. THE COMPUTER WILL DO THE REST.
GREAT.
THE ANGLE AND EXPOSURE ARE ALL AUTOMATIC NOW.
ALL WE HAVE TO DO NOW IS WAIT.
HMMM.
ASTRONOMY SURE IS BORING.
I WONDER IF THEY'VE GIVEN UP YET...
HUH?
AWESOME, SAATI!
WE'RE DEAD-ON HERE!
HMPH!
THEY'RE MOVING IT WITH THEIR HANDS?
DON'T YOU THINK...
?!
...YOU'RE JUST WASTING YOUR TIME?

NO MATTER WHAT YOU DO...
...YOU'LL NEVER MATCH MY TELESCOPE.
LOOK, IT TAKES MORE THAN JUST EQUIPMENT.
NOW QUIT BUGGING US, OKAY?
YOU KEEP SAYING THAT, BUT JUST WAIT UNTIL YOU SEE MY PICTURES.
YOU CAN BOW OUT GRACEFULLY NOW. NO HARD FEELINGS.
....
ARE YOU SAYING THERE'S NO CHANCE THAT YOU COULD LOSE?
OF COURSE NOT.
BUT IF I DO LOSE...
...I'LL LET YOU USE MY SUMMER HOME FOR THE WEEK.
OOH--I'LL EVEN BE YOUR MAID FOR THE DURATION!
SO JUST HANG IN THERE, NOW!
DAMN, THAT BITCH NEVER SHUTS UP.
MAYBE I SHOULD JUST GO BLOW UP HER CAR.

NO, TONI. THERE'S NO POINT IN THAT.
WE HAVE TO WIN FAIR AND SQUARE.
OKAY, IT'S ALMOST TIME.
SAATI, YOU READY?
READY!
EVEN SO, YOU'RE STILL AT A DIS-ADVANTAGE.
HMMM.
I'LL JUST ACCESS THEIR COMPUTER AND...
...MAKE IT SO THEY CAN'T GET A GOOD PICTURE.
MMMNN.
HUH?
THAT WAS SIMPLE. ALL I HAVE TO DO IS HIT CANCEL.
PIECE OF CAKE.
HUH?
!!
HASN'T ANYONE...
...HEARD OF AN EXTERMI-NATOR?!

AARGH!
ARRGH
SAY, WHAT'S GOING ON?
IS THAT MY OBSERVATORY THAT'S ON FIRE?!

THIS IS IT, EVERYBODY! ANY MOMENT NOW!!
NO--MY PICTURES!!
BINGO! TIME TO START THE EXPOSURE.

....

I HOPE THIS WORKS.
RIGHT NOW, THE LATEST FRAGMENT SHOULD BE HITTING JUPITER.

SAATI IS DOING HER PART...

...BUT THIS CAMERA DOESN'T HAVE A VIEWFINDER.
THERE'S NO WAY TO TELL IF JUPITER'S IN THE FRAME OR NOT.

MAN, JUST PRESSING THIS CABLE RELEASE...
...IS KILLING MY FINGERS.

BUT IF THIS PICTURE DOESN'T COME OUT RIGHT...
...IT'LL BE THE END OF THE ASTRONOMY CLUB. I HAVE TO STAY STRONG.

OH NO! HAS THE EXPLOSION ALREADY HAPPENED?
WHAT SHOULD I DO?

THAT'S IT! I'LL JUST USE MY ORIGINAL TELESCOPE!!
バーン
AT LEAST THE CAMERA IS BUILT IN.
あせあせ
あせあせ
LETS SEE, JUPITER IS THIS WAY.

HMM, I THINK I GOT IT.

OH GOD...

...MY HAND IS NUMB.

HUH? IT'S ONLY BEEN A COUPLE OF MINUTES?

HOW MUCH LONGER DO I HAVE TO DO THIS?

I JUST HOPE EVERYTHING IS OKAY.

I DON'T THINK I CAN FORGIVE MYSELF IF I SCREW THIS UP.

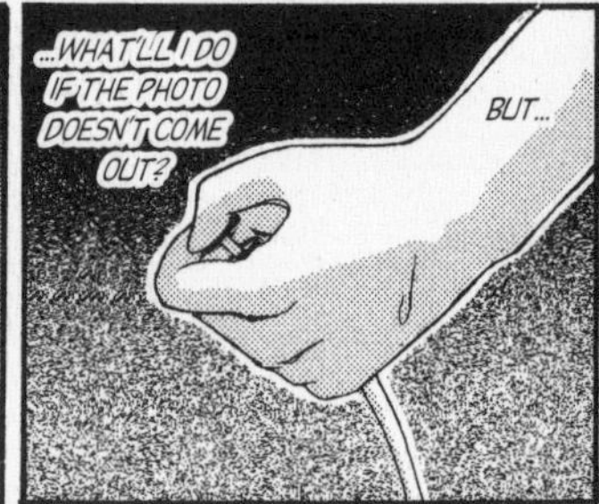

BUT...
...WHAT'LL I DO IF THE PHOTO DOESN'T COME OUT?

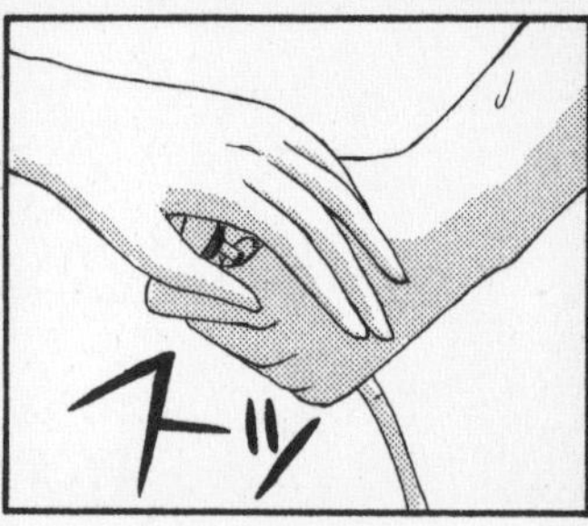

AHH...?

RELAX, HITOSHI-SAN.
I'M SURE EVERYTHING WILL BE FINE.

YOU'RE RIGHT.

I NEED TO HAVE FAITH...

...IN OUR STRENGTH.

AND IT'S TIME.
OKAY.
I'M RELEAS-ING THE SHUTTER NOW.
カシャ
ALRIGHTY, EVERYONE! WE HAVE A WINNER!

AND IN JUST A MOMENT, WE'LL SHOW YOU THAT LUCKY PHOTO!
HMM, COULD IT BE MINE?
DRUM ROLL, PLEASE!!
OOOHHH!!
ザワ
THAT'S AMAZING!
ザワ
THE COMPOSITION IS PERFECT.
WOW. WE CAN'T COM-PETE WITH THAT.
AND THE WINNER IS HITOSHI--
HUH?
HITOSHI KOBE!
YEAH, WE DID IT!!
ALL RIGHT, HITOSHI-SAN!

WAIT A MINUTE!
WHAT ABOUT MY PICTURES?!
MY EQUIPMENT WAS TEN TIMES BETTER THAN HITOSHI'S!
UM, AND YOUR NAME IS?
KIMIKA ASO!
AH, YOUR PICTURES WERE COMPLETELY BLACK AND UNEXPOSED.
I'M AFRAID YOU DIDN'T LET IN ENOUGH LIGHT.
NO WAY!
I USED THE FLASH THE WHOLE TIME!
UM, YEAH... USING THE FLASH IN ASTRONOMY PHOTOS IS A BIG NO-NO.
IT IS?!
The following night...
THAT OVER THERE IS CYGNUS, AND THAT'S LYRA.
AND THE ONE THAT'S REALLY BRIGHT...
...THAT'S THE NORTH STAR. IT'S LUCKY.
WOW.
HOW ROMANTIC.

BUT YOU KNOW WHAT? TO ME...
...YOU'LL ALWAYS BE...
MY LUCKY STAR.
AH.

WAAGGH!!
WHERE'D YOU GET *THAT* CHEESY LINE, HUH?!

JEEZ!
WHAT DO YOU WANT NOW, TONI?!

I FIGURE, AS LONG AS WE'RE STAYIN' HERE FOR FREE...
...WE OUGHTTA AT LEAST HAVE SOME FUN.

YOO-HOO, BIKINI GIRL!
IS DINNER READY YET?

SHUT UP AND BRING IT OUT YOURSELF!!
LOOK HERE, YOU'RE OUR MAID FOR THE WEEK AND THAT'S FINAL!
UGH, WE CAN'T TAKE HER ANY-WHERE.

▶To Be Continued

Originally published in 1994 in Weekly Shonen Magazine issues 26, 27 and 29 through 35.

Program.

Next Volume

In the next volume of A.I. Love You

New Friends...and New Enemies!

Toni's in trouble (again!), but this time the danger's greater than ever! Peter 4--the computer virus that almost claimed Saati's life--is back...and he's not alone. Hitoshi, Saati and Toni are put to the test in their first encounter with Peter 4's creator!

(No.20)

THOUGH PROGRAM TWENTY WOULD EVENTUALLY BECOME A SORT OF "OLDER SISTER" TO EVERYONE, SHE REMAINED A SHINING EXAMPLE OF A.I. TECHNOLOGY. THIS IS IN PART DUE TO THE FACT THAT SHE WAS PROGRAMMED USING ASSEMBLY LANGUAGE, THE FASTEST PROGRAMMING LANGUAGE AVAILABLE. HOWEVER, UNLIKE SAATI, SHE DOES NOT HAVE A FEEDBACK FUNCTION AND IS THUS UNABLE TO LEARN OR GROW. OVERALL, TWENTY HAS VERY FEW BUGS AND RARELY MALFUNCTIONS. IF *A.I. LOVE YOU* HAD BEEN CONCEIVED AS A CYBER PUNK NARRATIVE, TWENTY WOULD MOST DEFINITELY HAVE APPEARED AS A SOLDIER. UNFORTUNATELY, SINCE THIS IS A ROMANTIC COMEDY, SHE DOESN'T STAND OUT THAT MUCH.

PROGRAM No.20

3 SIZE DATE

B:86

W:59

H:88

Cover Illustration Gallery

The Cover Illustration from the April 4, 1995 issue of Weekly Shonen Magazine

The Original Cover Art from the First Release of Volume 2

The Original Cover Art from the First Release of Volume 4

ALSO AVAILABLE FROM TOKYOPOP®

PRINCESS AI
PSYCHIC ACADEMY
RAGNAROK
RAVE MASTER
REALITY CHECK
REBIRTH
REBOUND
REMOTE
RISING STARS OF MANGA
SABER MARIONETTE J
SAILOR MOON
SAINT TAIL
SAIYUKI
SAMURAI DEEPER KYO
SAMURAI GIRL REAL BOUT HIGH SCHOOL
SCRYED
SEIKAI TRILOGY, THE
SGT. FROG
SHAOLIN SISTERS
SHIRAHIME-SYO: SNOW GODDESS TALES
SHUTTERBOX
SKULL MAN, THE
SMUGGLER
SNOW DROP
SORCERER HUNTERS
STONE
SUIKODEN III
SUKI
THREADS OF TIME
TOKYO BABYLON
TOKYO MEW MEW
TRAMPS LIKE US
TREASURE CHESS
UNDER THE GLASS MOON
VAMPIRE GAME
VISION OF ESCAFLOWNE, THE
WARRIORS OF TAO
WILD ACT
WISH
WORLD OF HARTZ
X-DAY
ZODIAC P.I.

NOVELS

CLAMP SCHOOL PARANORMAL INVESTIGATORS
KARMA CLUB
SAILOR MOON
SLAYERS

ART BOOKS

ART OF CARDCAPTOR SAKURA
ART OF MAGIC KNIGHT RAYEARTH, THE
PEACH: MIWA UEDA ILLUSTRATIONS

ANIME GUIDES

COWBOY BEBOP
GUNDAM TECHNICAL MANUALS
SAILOR MOON SCOUT GUIDES

TOKYOPOP KIDS

STRAY SHEEP

CINE-MANGA™

ALADDIN
ASTRO BOY
CARDCAPTORS
CONFESSIONS OF A TEENAGE DRAMA QUEEN
DUEL MASTERS
FAIRLY ODDPARENTS, THE
FAMILY GUY
FINDING NEMO
G.I. JOE SPY TROOPS
JACKIE CHAN ADVENTURES
JIMMY NEUTRON: BOY GENIUS, THE ADVENTURES OF
KIM POSSIBLE
LILO & STITCH
LIZZIE MCGUIRE
LIZZIE MCGUIRE MOVIE, THE
MALCOLM IN THE MIDDLE
POWER RANGERS: NINJA STORM
SHREK 2
SPONGEBOB SQUAREPANTS
SPY KIDS 2
SPY KIDS 3-D: GAME OVER
TEENAGE MUTANT NINJA TURTLES
THAT'S SO RAVEN
TRANSFORMERS: ARMADA
TRANSFORMERS: ENERGON

For more information visit www.TOKYOPOP.com

02.03.04T

TOKYOPOP
Do you remember your first love?
She remembers you!
藍より青し
あい
あお
AI YORI AOSHI™
Available Now
OT
OLDER TEEN
AGE 16+
©1998 Kou Fumizuki. ©2004 TOKYOPOP Inc. All rights reserved.
www.TOKYOPOP.com

STOP!

This is the back of the book. You wouldn't want to spoil a great ending!

This book is printed "manga-style," in the authentic Japanese right-to-left format. Since none of the artwork has been flipped or altered, readers get to experience the story just as the creator intended. You've been asking for it, so TOKYOPOP® delivered: authentic, hot-off-the-press, and far more fun!

DIRECTIONS

If this is your first time reading manga-style, here's a quick guide to help you understand how it works.

It's easy... just start in the top right panel and follow the numbers. Have fun, and look for more 100% authentic manga from TOKYOPOP®!